THE ESSENTIAL STUDENT GUIDE

Starting University

What to Expect • How to Prepare • Go and Enjoy

by Melissa Scallan

Edited by Louise Salmon • Design and Illustrations by Molly Shields

To my family

What students say about **The Essential Student Guide - *Starting University***

"Everything about going to university is made so simple. There were things I hadn't thought of doing and the double checklist is great!"

"I loved it and felt there was nothing missing. My mum and I wished we could have had this book because she felt we were doing it blind"

"I really enjoyed reading this book. I LOVE that both sides (positive and negative) of social media are highlighted. And listing the different places you can reach out to if you're really struggling is great - it highlights that there are lots of options!"

"I found the chapter on money very useful and it's given me lots of ideas on how to save money and spend wisely."

What parents say about **The Essential Student Guide - *Starting University***

"So many things to think about in such an easy to read format. I love the checklist and ticking it off twice - great idea to help feel in control of jumping off the precipice into the unknown. I wish I had this book when I went off to university - it would have made my first year so much easier!"

"It's very easy to read and digest. Really nicely presented with not too much information on each page to overwhelm you. The link to the website that shows how much they pay in rent at each university and how much they spend on food etc is a great idea. It's useful to get an idea of monthly outgoings and that looks spot on!"

"This book is helpful on so many counts. I'm a planner and the timeline is really useful in telling me what my daughter needs to do and by what date. Also, the money section prepares us for how much we'll need to give her and how much she'll need to pay back when she graduates. It's brilliant: one place to go to for everything we need to know."

First published in Great Britain in 2019 by Katelli Publishing
www.katelli.co.uk

British Library Cataloguing-in-Publication Data: a catalogue record for this book is
available from the British Library
Paperback ISBN 978-1-9161027-0-5

The information in this book has been compiled by way of general guidance only. The
author and the publisher shall have no liability or responsibility to any person or entity
regarding any loss, damage, disruption or injury incurred, or alleged to have incurred,
directly or indirectly by the information or suggestions contained in this book.

All brand names and product names used in this book are trade names, service
marks and trade or registered trademarks of their respective owners. The author is
not associated with any product or vendor mentioned in this book other than where
explicitly stated.

Printed in the United Kingdom

Contents

8 **Staying Safe at University 103**

Introduction

You're getting ready for university - fantastic!

You're about to embark on one of the most exciting, life-changing phases of your life. Over the next few years you'll enjoy a range of new experiences, you'll make good friends, you'll become more independent and you'll also become more knowledgeable. And you won't be on your own. In 2017-18, over 600,000 students enrolled as first year undergraduates at universities in the UK.

The Essential Student Guide - Starting University is designed to help you by offering practical, easy-to-read, useful advice on what to expect, how to prepare, what to take with you and how to deal with many of the new experiences you'll be facing during your first year at a UK university.

The guide is not only for students living away from home for the first time, but it also includes information and advice for everyone in their first year at university. You'll find suggestions on essentials to pack, from bedding to first aid kits and basic kitchen implements, alongside advice on friendships and relationships, nights out and staying safe, food and laundry. From Freshers' Week to study strategies and finances to mental health, it's all here. And there's a chapter for your parents too.

If you're moving to university, suggestions of what to take can be found throughout the book. You won't need all of it and you might want to add to it, but it will give you a good basis from which to start. The list approach - 'got' and 'packed' - focuses the mind, removes some of the uncertainty around what to take, and gives you the pleasure of ticking things off (twice).

In compiling this guide, I reviewed the information provided by a wide range of organisations including UK universities; sixth form and further education colleges; student forums; higher education admissions, regulatory, news and analysis organisations; financial information providers; news organisations;

physical and mental health service providers; drug, smoking and alcohol advisory services; Government and affiliated organisations; and commercial providers of goods and services to students.

It was crucial that I heard directly from students themselves, so I also carried out a programme of research amongst Freshers - first year undergraduate students - who were attending UK universities on a full-time basis. The research took the form of an online semi-structured questionnaire, filled in on an anonymous basis, and undertaken during the middle-end of their first term at university. More than sixty students responded, sharing the highs and lows of going to university and the advice they would give to new students. Where appropriate, and with their permission, I've included their wise, witty and poignant comments throughout this guide: it informs the content and brings the student experience to life.

I also paid attention to observations and comments made by parents of new students, taking note of their concerns, experiences and recommendations.

This book is packed with information, advice and lists. I hope you find it helpful. Please do email me if you think I've missed something crucial, if you have a good suggestion, would like to comment on the book or would like updates. I'd be very happy to hear from you: melissa@theessentialstudentguide.co.uk

Good luck at university!

Melissa
June 2019

Instagram: TheEssentialStudentGuide
Facebook: TheEssentialStudentGuide
Website: TheEssentialStudentGuide.co.uk

Notes:

- For the sake of readability, I've used the term 'university' to refer to all higher education providers, 'A levels' to refer to all pre-higher education exams, 'undergraduates' to refer to those attending higher education institutions studying for their first degree or similar, and 'parents' to include parents, carers and guardians

- Dates, links to websites, telephone numbers and references to the EU were correct at the time of printing. See End Notes for links to websites and licences

- Where I've mentioned brands or organisations, it's because I think the product or service is particularly useful or helpful. I'd be happy to hear from you if you have a recommendation of a product or service - and what makes it so good

- The Augar Review into post-18 education (May 2019) made a number of recommendations but it remains to be seen which, if any, will be implemented

Countdown to Leaving

This seasonal timeline indicates what generally happens and when during the academic year prior to going to university to study as a full-time undergraduate student in the UK. There may be individual differences that reflect your personal circumstances, the course or the university.

Additional elements such as admission tests, interviews, auditions, preparation of a portfolio or early deadlines, may apply depending on the course you're applying for or the university you're applying to.

It's important to check specific dates, deadlines and individual requirements with each university and course you're considering, with your school or college, and with UCAS: the Universities and Colleges Admissions Service.

Autumn (normally Year 13) . . . .

- Attend university open days for any universities you're considering that you didn't see during Year 12
- Edit/finalise your personal statement
    - This is an important part of your university application and it's where you explain why you'd like to study a particular course or subject and what skills or experiences you have in that area. It also tells the university about you e.g. your ambitions, your interests, your achievements, why you're suitable to study at their university
    - You only write one personal statement: the same one gets sent to each course you apply for. So don't mention universities by name - or course names, if they vary
    - Don't be tempted to plagiarise: UCAS uses sophisticated computer software to detect copied text
- Give your school/college enough time to read your application, check your qualifications, write and attach your reference
- Have you considered other degree options? E.g. a sponsored degree, a degree apprenticeship or an accelerated degree

- Choose up to five courses to apply for
  - This is the limit under the UK system
  - Be realistic in your course choices. Your school or college will tell you your predicted grades. Compare these to the published grades that universities normally require from students to study specific courses. You should apply for courses you have a good chance of getting a place on
  - Choose courses with higher and lower grade requirements so that you'll have an insurance/back-up option
- UCAS normally starts to accept applications in September for most undergraduate courses
  - Don't delay as universities start sending out offers within weeks of receiving applications
- Any course at the universities of Oxford and Cambridge and for most courses in medicine, veterinary medicine/science, dentistry, and music courses at conservatoires require early application to UCAS (the deadline is normally October)
- Some universities and some courses may invite you to interview or sit their own admission test

Winter ....

- Start to receive decisions
- January is normally the UCAS deadline for the majority of university applications (note the deadline for early application above). It's possible to apply after this date but course choices may be limited and decision times will change
- If you included five choices on your application but have not received any offers - or you declined the offers you received - you can normally apply to UCAS Extra in February for an additional course

Spring

- Continue to receive decisions from universities
- Visit universities (again) on offer holder open days:
  universities that have made you offers may invite you to visit. The day
  normally includes an introduction to the department, information about
  your course, a tour of the department/campus, taster lectures (which
  parents can attend), and meeting staff and current students
- Accept or decline your offers; normally keeping a firm (first choice) and
  insurance (back-up) offer
- If you firmly accept an unconditional offer (where the university place is
  not dependent on achieving certain A level grades)
  - You're normally committed to going to that university so you can't
    make an insurance choice, be entered into Clearing or Adjustment
  - It's really important that you keep working and get the best A level
    results you can
- Apply for university accommodation, if required
- Apply for student loans, and government grants and allowances,
  if required and if you're eligible. Investigate other grants, awards,
  scholarships and bursaries

Summer

- Sit your exams - good luck!
- Start practising - or improving - useful life skills,
  particularly if you're moving away from home for university e.g. cooking,
  laundry, supermarket shopping
- Work, work, work - save, save, save! Build up your savings by undertaking
  paid work
- Results Day. This is particularly important if your place at university is
  conditional on you achieving certain A level grades
  - Depending on what you're studying, schools and colleges will
    receive results on different dates - check when your results will be
    available

- UCAS Track updates at 8am on Results Day showing whether you've been accepted onto your firm or insurance course (if no decisions are showing, contact your universities)
- If a place on a course is offered: accept or decline
- If you didn't meet the conditions of your offer, the university may still offer you a place, or a place on an alternative course
- If you've not received any university offers - or none you wanted - then you can apply for a course that still has spaces through UCAS Clearing
- If you receive your results prior to A level Results Day you can enter Clearing early since it opens in July. However, most Clearing vacancies won't be published until August so you'll need to wait until then if you want to see the full selection of places that are available
- If you performed better than expected - met and exceeded conditions for your firm choice - you might consider applying for an alternative course through UCAS Adjustment
- Fingers crossed: you're getting ready to go to university!

"Don't stress. No one knows what they're doing or how things are going to pan out."

(Female, age 18)

1

How Are You Feeling?

The days are flying by and your first day at university is getting closer. How are you feeling?

Can't Wait!

Hopefully you're pretty excited about starting university.

- If you've attended the same school or lived in the same place for a long time, you could be completely ready to experience a new environment

- If you're moving away to go to university, maybe you're keen to leave home: to strike out on your own, to experience freedom, be independent

- Perhaps you loved what you saw during the university open days or what other people have told you about university life

- Maybe you're excited about your course or you're keen to take the next steps towards your future career

- If you're not too happy at home, school, college or work then going to university could be a great move

- Or perhaps you're just looking forward to a new beginning

And if you've taken a gap year, travelled, worked or you're used to looking after yourself - managing your money, getting yourself to places, doing your own shopping, cooking, laundry and cleaning - then, great! That's one part of the student experience that many Freshers find challenging - and you've already got it nailed.

Bit Worried About Leaving Home

Perhaps you're in the sixth form or attending a further education college, living at home but on the verge of moving out. If your parents help with many aspects of day-to-day living, and you're leaving home to go to university, you might have some concerns about being away from them.

It's possible your parents help you with:

- Food: making healthy choices, buying it, cooking it, clearing it away. No thought of food may have passed through your mind other than scouring cupboards when you're starving and preferring some foods over others

- Clothes: buying most of your 'essentials' such as jackets, jeans, trainers and underwear. They might also collect those clothes from the floordrobe, wash them, hang them out, iron them and return them to your room

- Transport: if you live somewhere that doesn't have very good public transport, they may be driving you places. Even if you can drive and have access to a car, you might still avail yourself of that great service

- Cleaning: providing you with clean bed sheets and towels and replacing bathroom essentials when they run out. And, even if you're responsible for your bedroom (or your part of it), they probably keep the rest of the home clean and tidy

- Bank of Mum and Dad: it's likely that, in addition to providing your bed and board, they might give you an allowance, pay or contribute towards a phone, a computer, travel costs, clothes, school-related costs, health, eye and dental costs. They might pay when things need fixing and lend you money when you don't have your card or cash on you (do you sometimes forget to pay it back?)

- And hopefully they're supportive: listening to you when you feel like talking, making reasonable suggestions that you may or may not take, and picking you up when you're feeling down

If this sounds like you, then you might have concerns around:

- Sticking to a budget: you might never have had to restrict your spending or divide up your money into things like rent, food, travel and laundry

- Making household decisions on things like food, cleaning and tackling clothes washing

- Making decisions without using your parents as a sounding board

- Being apart from them for any length of time

- You might even be worried about how your parents will cope without you

Other Possible Concerns

You might also have some other concerns, such as:

- If you're moving away then you might be wondering whether you'll like your accommodation and who your flatmates will be

- You're undoubtedly hoping you'll quickly find friends

- What about a girlfriend or boyfriend? If you're travelling some distance, you might be leaving someone important behind. Or perhaps you're hoping to find someone

- Given the cost and importance of going to university, you might be wondering whether you've chosen the right course, the right university, the right location and if you'll enjoy it

- And what if you're an international student? In 2017-18, 16% of full-time undergraduate students and a huge 54% of full-time postgraduate students were from outside the UK. If you're moving to the UK to study then you might also have a range of concerns such as being geographically distant from your support network, possibly having to study and socialise in a foreign language, and maybe understanding and adopting different cultural norms. You might be feeling the weight of your family's expectations, worried about the impact of Brexit and you're undoubtedly hoping that people - other students and university staff - will be friendly, welcoming and supportive

So, it's not unreasonable that you might be experiencing some anxiety. This book can't take away all those worries - which are quite natural and part of the process of helping you prepare for change - but, by providing you with practical advice and information, it can help to minimise some of your fears.

2

Important Things To Do Before The Start Of Term

This is a pretty comprehensive list of things to do. Don't worry if it doesn't all get done before you start - lots of things can be sorted out once you arrive at university.

All New Students

- Set up your student bank account

    - Student bank accounts aren't compulsory but they do tend to offer extra features that are helpful such as fee-free and interest-free overdraft facilities. They may offer you a free rail card, coach card or gift card as an enticement to bank with them
    - You can start this process early: if you apply to university through UCAS Undergraduate, you'll be issued status codes which some banks use to confirm your eligibility for their student accounts
    - Once you have your bank account, set up online banking so you can check your balance and you can contact the bank if (when) you mislay your bank card

"I lost my debit card. It could be in one of two nightclubs or three taxis...."
(Female, age 18)

- International students: you may only be able to set up a UK bank account once you arrive in the UK

- Student loans

  - If you're from the UK or the EU, if you're eligible and if you require them, you can apply for student loans: the tuition fee loan and the maintenance loan
  - You can start this process early (normally from March of the year you're intending to go to university) and you don't need a confirmed place to apply
  - It can take up to six week for loans to come through so, if you want the money in your bank account when you start the course, it's best not to delay applying. However, you can apply for loans up to 9 months after the first day of the academic year for your course
  - You may be eligible for additional Government-provided financial support. You can apply for this when you apply for student loans
  - If you're eligible, you can get a maintenance loan whether living in halls of residences, in private accommodation or if you're living at home
  - Go to www.gov.uk/student-finance and follow the links if you're from Scotland, Wales or Northern Ireland
  - Students from outside the EU (apart from in certain specific circumstances), aren't eligible for these loans, and you'll need to find another way to fund your studies

- Finances in general: think about any alternative/additional payments

  - It's possible that any maintenance loan may not be sufficient even to cover accommodation costs so you should consider other ways you could fund your time at university (read Chapter 7: Money)

- If your parents are contributing, then agree how much and how often they will transfer money. It may help with budgeting to receive money on a weekly basis (read Chapter 7: Money or Chapter 9: Parents - for a suggestion on parental contribution)
- Talk to your parents or teachers about managing your finances e.g. budgeting, bills, ways of saving money, overdrafts
- Try to find or increase your paid work in order to build up your savings. Being a student - whether it's socialising with your new friends or managing living costs - is nearly always more expensive than you anticipate. According to student news site The Tab, Freshers' Week alone - with club entry, pre-drinks, taxis, drinking, fancy dress, hangover food, society sign-ups and the weekly shop - can come to over £400 (and this was in 2015)

- When you receive written confirmation of your place from the university, read through the letter

  - There may be specific things you need to do e.g. you may need to send the university proof of your qualifications
  - Accept your place at the university. You'll then begin receiving information from the university such as your student ID card, registration details, course or module choices, accommodation details, your university email address, Freshers' or Welcome Week information

- Get ready for the start of term

  - Read through any information sent by your department - there may be materials they'd like you to prepare in advance, books to read or equipment you need to buy
  - Look online and see where things are e.g. your term-time address, your academic department, the leisure centre/sports facilities, the Student Union, your nearest supermarket, medical centre, support services

- Figure out how you're going to get to and from your classes e.g. bike, bus, walk, train

- Social media

  - Upload or update your social media accounts e.g. Facebook, Instagram and Snapchat. That's how most students connect and communicate
  - Most universities have moderated social media accounts for new students. When your place is confirmed, go online and find your future hall/block/corridor/flatmates, discover people studying the same course, and get in touch with clubs and societies you might be interested in joining. Don't be shy: join in. Everyone's new and keen to make friends. It'll make the first day so much better to know names, faces and a bit about people ahead of time

- General health

  - Make sure your vaccinations are up-to-date e.g. MMR, meningitis ACWY. You'll be coming into contact with a lot of new people, some of whom may unknowingly be carriers of illnesses
  - Diarise booking a flu jab in the autumn, especially if you're an 'at risk' person e.g. asthmatic

- If you have any mental or physical health needs

  - Tell your home therapist/GP about your plans so they can help prepare you for the transition
  - They can also let the university know in advance about your needs to ensure speedy access to services/continuity of care
  - You may be eligible for additional financial support e.g. Disabled Students Allowance. You can apply for this when you apply for student loans. Allow yourself time to make the application since you might need to provide evidence

- See the 'Important Documents Checklist', at the end of this chapter for vital information to gather before the start of term

- Sort out your essentials and stationery – see the lists at the end of this chapter for suggestions

- Read this book and talk to other people who've gone to university

If You're Living Away from Home

- If university accommodation is offered, accept (or reject) the offer. If you reject it, follow the university's advice on what you need to do to find alternative accommodation

- If you need private accommodation, contact the university accommodation service for advice

- Undertake all the necessary admin

  - Write down your term-time address and look up how to get there
  - Confirm your moving-in day and time, if this is offered
  - See what's provided in your hall/flat/room so you know what to take
  - Pay your deposit (usually up to one month's rent)
  - Set up a standing order to pay your rent (and possibly household bills, if not included in your rent)
  - Read Chapter 3: Your New Accommodation

- General health

  - Students normally register with their university GP so you need to gather various pieces of information to give to the university surgery/health centre e.g. your NHS number, your home GP's details, any medication you regularly take, your immunisation history (which you can normally get from your home GP)

- Visit your home GP and get a month's worth of any repeat/regular medication so you're fully stocked up until you register with the university GP
- Visit your home dentist and optician and get any work done before you leave

If you're unwell when you're away from your university GP e.g. during a visit home, you can request an appointment with the nearest GP practice. You can receive emergency treatment for 14 days but after that you'll have to register as a temporary resident or permanent patient

- If you have any mental or physical health needs, let the university know in advance. They may allow you to move into your term-time accommodation a few days early so you can settle and make contact with student support services

- Gather together everything you need to take with you (see the lists within each chapter)

If, on arrival at university, you discover you don't have something, seriously don't worry: chances are you can get it from a local shop, order it online, borrow it or improvise

- If you've bought anything new to take with you

  - Open items up and check them, especially anything electrical
  - Remove any packaging - this will reduce the space required for transporting them

- Investigate whether you need any specific contents insurance

  - A university hall of residence might provide contents insurance but this might be restricted to items lost or damaged within a locked room or within the hall
  - Additional insurance might be necessary for expensive possessions such as a bike, musical instrument, phone or laptop

- Decide whether or not you need a television licence and, if so, buy it

  - A licence is needed to download or watch BBC programmes on demand, including catch up TV, on BBC iPlayer. You'll also need a licence if you're watching or recording live TV on any channel
  - However, you're covered by a valid licence at your parents' address if the device you're using to watch television is powered by its own internal batteries, is not plugged into the mains and is not connected to an aerial

- Food and drink

  - If you don't prepare meals very often, practise cooking some quick and tasty meals from scratch

"Start thinking about day-to-day life before you go then it won't come as a shock.... Every now and then just think 'If I had to eat something now and my parents weren't around, what would I do?'"
(Male, age 20)

  - Read Chapter 5: Food & Drink - suggestions of what to eat and some easy recipes
  - If you don't already shop for food, do some supermarket shopping as this will be useful practice for when you're on your own. For example, you'll see how supermarkets are laid out, how to find things and what they cost

- If your nearest term-time supermarket is far away, you could practice ordering food online so you're familiar with its service e.g. learn how to navigate the website, see the actual cost of items and the delivery cost, and see how frequently it delivers to your area (you can add your term-time address and see the impact on frequency)
- Read how to 'Shop Savvy' in Chapter 7

- If you don't already do it, learn how to do laundry

  - At the very least you need to know how to use the washing machine
  - Read Chapter 4: Laundry

- See what taxi services operate in your university area

  - Your university may have a list of recommended taxi firms
  - If it's an online service, and you're not already a customer, you could try using it so you're familiar with how the service works
  - Taking a taxi might sound extravagant but sharing a ride with friends can be as little as £1/person

- If you're an international student, in addition to the above, there may be other things that you need to arrange in advance, such as:

  - Visa
  - Passport
  - Health insurance and/or European Health Insurance Card and/or pay the health surcharge
  - Travel insurance
  - Proof of finance
  - Proof of address: in the UK and your home address
  - Confirmation of acceptance of studies
  - A SIM card to make local calls from your phone

- Set up web-based accounts so you can make calls for free over the internet (except for any web access costs) when you and the other person are both online and using the same service e.g. WhatsApp, FaceTime, Skype
- Investigate what your university organises specifically for its international students, such as welcome and orientation events, International Halls, dedicated social media, student welfare, language lessons or a general support service

DOCUMENT CHECKLIST

	Got	Packed
Offer letter from the university		
Term-time accommodation address and how to get there		
Accommodation tenancy agreement		
Campus map		
Exam certificates		
Student loan/funding details		
Bank account details: regular and student accounts		
Any bursary/scholarship/sponsorship/grant/award documentation		

Health information including:

	Got	Packed
Home GP details: name, address, telephone number		
NHS number		
Medication taken regularly: name, dosage, frequency, when to be renewed, etc		
Copy of immunisation record		
Any current health information e.g. copy of glasses prescription		
ID in the form of driving licence/provisional licence/passport		
National Insurance details		
Any insurance documents/details		
TV licence, if necessary		

Foreign students might also need:

	Got	Packed
Visa		
Passport		
Birth certificate		
Travel documents		
Health insurance		
Travel insurance		
Funding documents		

ESSENTIALS CHECKLIST

	Got	Packed
Phone plus charging cable		
Laptop/computer plus charging cable		
A 3-port USB charger is useful e.g. IKEA KOPPLA		
Portable battery for your phone plus charging cable		
Earphones (plus charging cable if Bluetooth)		
Printer plus charging cable, ink cartridges and printer paper		
USB memory stick		
Ear plugs		
Cash		
Debit card		
Rail/coach card		
Student ID card		
Store/loyalty cards		
Diary/calendar (academic diaries start in September)		
Plug extension cable		
Foreign students will need plug adapters, SIM card		

STATIONERY CHECKLIST

	Got	Packed
Files/folders		
Pads of paper of various types e.g. A4, ruled, graph, plain		
Textbooks		
Pens		
Pencils		
Sticky tape in a dispenser		
Scissors		
Highlighters		
Ruler		
Hole punch		
Pencil sharpener		
Eraser		
Paper clips		
Sticky notes		
Sticky tack		
Calculator		
Plastic wallets		
Course-specific items		
Pencil case		

3

Living Away From Home: Your New Accommodation

Freedom!

The majority of undergraduate students, who study in the UK, live away from home during term time. In 2017-18, some 60% of undergraduate students lived in university halls, private-sector halls and in other rental accommodation.

When I asked the first year students in my research what they liked most about being at university, living away from home was one of the most common answers they gave. They enjoy the freedom that comes from no longer living under their parents' roof - and not having to abide by their parents' rules. Enjoy!

"The freedom and independence to do what I want, when I want"
(Male, age 19)

"Social aspects, nights out, freedom to look after yourself"
(Female, age 18)

"Freedom to live as you wish"
(Male, age 20)

"The freedom of living away from home but also having a support network, the social life and the course"
(Female, age 19)

"You get to make your own rules, especially when it comes to going out and drinking"
(Male, age 18)

Typical First Year Accommodation

If you're living away from home, your choice of accommodation will generally fall into one of the following three options:

- University hall of residence
- Private hall of residence
- Privately rented accommodation

University Halls of Residence

It's good to visit a few halls of residence during university open days to get an idea of how they're set up

- Halls of residences are often quite similar: usually flats of varying sizes with multiple single-occupation study bedrooms with either en suites or shared bathrooms and there's often a communal kitchen/dining area. Occasionally there may be shared study bedrooms. Rooms in older halls might be situated off long corridors

- WiFi is normally included and there's usually a launderette on site. Services and facilities provided in halls vary widely between, and within, universities

- There's usually an on-site warden - either a member of staff or an older student - who can offer advice, support and possibly first aid

- Rooms in halls tend to be the most popular option. They're usually close to the university, the rent tends to include utilities (and sometimes food), which makes it easier to budget, and you'd be living with other students from your university

- If you choose the catered option, there might be a dining room where meals are served or there may be various places around the university where you can eat, using a pre-paid card. Meals may not be provided three times a day, seven days a week so you may want to bring some cutlery, crockery and basic cooking equipment

Private Halls of Residence

Private halls of residence are normally owned and managed by a private provider that specialises in student accommodation

- The accommodation is often similar in style to university halls of residences i.e. flats or rooms with shared facilities

- Sometimes the facilities may be newer or more luxurious than those found in the university halls. If the facilities are better, it's likely the rent will also be higher

- Check what's included in your rent e.g. utilities

- You may be living with students attending other local universities

Privately Rented Accommodation

You may have applied for university accommodation but not been allocated a room or you may simply prefer to live in privately rented accommodation

- Contact the university accommodation service for advice since it normally helps students with privately rented accommodation. The department may:
  - Provide a list of letting agents, private landlords or flat share lists
  - Identify which are the popular student areas
  - Give advice on current rent levels and paying deposits
  - Offer information on housing regulation and other aspects of a private sector tenancy e.g. gas safety certificate, the rent deposit scheme, registering for council tax exemption
  - Offer a contract-checking service

- You should always try to visit the property in person. Amongst other things, you can check its condition, see how long it takes you get to the university during rush hour and speak to existing tenants

- You normally pay your rent on a monthly basis (in advance). Utilities, e.g. gas and electricity, are usually paid separately

Applying for University and Private Halls of Residences

Check when you can apply for accommodation; often you can apply once you've made the university your firm (first) choice

- Some universities allow applications where they're the insurance (back-up) option

- Don't wait to apply. Universities tend to allocate places on a first come, first served basis and spaces in popular accommodation tend to fill up quickly

- You normally identify your top three or four preferred halls from a list - with your choices based on factors such as weekly cost, whether it has an en suite, whether it's catered or self-catered, distance from the university or faculty, whether you have any specific preferences/requirements

- Many universities guarantee a place in halls to first year students

You may be allocated a room in a hall that you've not had the opportunity to see in advance. Some universities have more accommodation options than you could reasonably see or you may be going to university through Clearing. Don't worry too much as the accommodation options tend to be fairly similar to each other

How is Accommodation Allocated?

Although some universities allow you to go online and select a specific room in a hall from a list of what's available, it's more common for universities to allocate accommodation based on its own algorithms, whilst taking into account your preferences or needs.

Much of the information below is based on research undertaken by the BBC in 2018 to identify how universities allocate rooms in halls of residences.

- Some universities actively mix up students with regard to factors such as gender, age, religious beliefs, nationality, faculty, school type - even setting percentage targets for the different types of student. Similarly, some universities have a policy to separate students from the same school or college
  - They reason that a valuable part of going to university is that students learn to mix with, and get to know, people whose lives and backgrounds are different to their own

- Some universities group Freshers with similar personality characteristics in order to ease the transition into university life. You might be asked about personality and lifestyle factors e.g. whether you're outgoing or reserved; an early-riser or night bird; a smoker or whether you drink alcohol; whether you're a vegetarian; tidy; sporty; like clubbing, etc

- This approach suggests that if you're similar to your flatmates it's easier to connect with them, you'll experience less conflict, you'll settle more quickly and be less homesick

If the university asks you to fill in a questionnaire, be honest about your personality and lifestyle factors as this increases the likelihood of being grouped with people who you'll feel comfortable living with

- Some universities allow students to request accommodation: either by selecting a specific room or requesting a room in a hall, according to what the university can offer
  - This might include applying to share with existing friends; requesting a room in alcohol-free halls or halls that have quiet areas; single-sex flats or halls; an LGBTQ+ community; by vegan/vegetarian/halal requirements; by nationality; by age; within a 'green' community

- And if you have a particular need for a certain type of accommodation, universities normally make available some accommodation to serve students with specific requirements e.g. if you have a child, have a particular mental or physical requirement, are estranged and therefore need year-round accommodation, have a carer who lives with you

- Finally, some universities state all accommodation is randomly allocated

Unhappy with Your Accommodation?

If you don't like your accommodation, speak to the university accommodation service. They'll be able to advise you on your options and, where available, offer alternative accommodation.

If you've already moved into a hall of residence, speak to the warden who may be able to resolve any issues. Whether in a hall or in a private residence there may be a fee to pay in order to break the contract and you may have to find someone to take your room. This, and any other information, should be in your tenancy agreement.

Your Study Bedroom

Whether moving into halls or privately rented accommodation, you're likely to be moving into a single room that will be your bedroom and study for the coming year.

It's likely to be simply furnished with a bed, mattress, mattress cover, bedside table, desk, chair, shelves, curtains, pin board and bin. Check the inventory as accommodation varies.

- Bedding
    - You usually provide your own bedding including pillows
    - You're likely to have limited storage so you could take just one set of bedding that you would wash and tumble dry on the same day
    - Include two sets of pillow cases so you can change these more regularly
    - Check the size of your bed in advance so you know what size fitted sheet and how many pillows to bring. Even if you have a single bed, take a double duvet to wrap yourself up in
    - Some universities sell bedding packs or suggest specialist private companies who can kit out your bedroom, your kitchen and bathroom - they deliver ready-made student packs directly to your halls to coincide with your arrival. UniKitOut (www.unikitout. com) works in partnership with over 160 universities and private housing providers and can deliver anywhere in the UK. If you apply the discount code TESG10 at the checkout, you'll receive a 10% saving off anything featured on the UniKitOut website (as a partner of UniKitOut, I receive a small commission when you apply the TESG10 discount code)

- A mattress cover/protector, if it's not provided, is a good idea. It's hygienic and helps to ensure your mattress stays fresh and clean
- A mattress topper (or a piece of foam the size of your mattress) provides extra cushioning and can make a bed more comfy

- Clothes and accessories
  - Bring enough clothes - especially underwear - so you can last at least a week (if not two) without needing to do laundry
  - Bring dressing-up clothes as fancy dress parties are common. Include a single, white, flat bed sheet, belt and safety pins for the inevitable toga party
  - If your hall hosts formal dinners then you should bring smart/ evening wear
  - Transport your clothes on their hangers in large bags so they'll be ready to hang when you arrive
  - Your first term takes you into winter so pack warm clothes
  - Pack flip flops for wearing in shared kitchens, bathrooms and leisure centre changing rooms

- Create your own first aid kit; it's cheaper than buying a ready-made one and it will be filled with the things you know you'll actually use

- Bring a door stop to prop your door open when you're in. It shows that you're welcoming and people can stop by and say hello

- Large under-bed storage boxes with lids are a good idea e.g. IKEA GIMSE. You're likely to have limited storage so this is where you could put things you rarely use

- You can create hanging shelves inside your wardrobe for extra storage e.g. IKEA SKUBB

- Bring accessories from home to decorate your room e.g. cushions, photos, fairy lights, rug, potted plant

- A full-size clothes horse/airer is useful for items that can't be tumbled and/or to save on drying costs. If you're moving into a hall of residence, there may be a drying room so you may not need a full size airer. A radiator airer for small items is also useful

- A sleeping bag is handy for when you have a friend staying over: single beds are common in student accommodation and there's not a lot of room for two

- A laundry bag with compartments for different shades of clothing is useful

- See the study/bedroom, personal/hygiene, first aid and other useful stuff checklists at the end of this chapter for suggestions of what to bring with you

On arrival check the room/inventory thoroughly, photograph any damages/ missing items and inform the accommodation management

Kitchen

Whether you're self-catering or being catered for, you'll probably have access to a shared kitchen where you normally have to provide everything you might need (but do check the inventory since some are well-equipped).

- Even if you choose the catered option, there'll be times when you don't want to go out for food so you might want to bring some basic crockery, cookware and ingredients for breakfasts, late night snacks and easy meals

- At minimum, bring mugs, glasses, tea, coffee, soft drinks, biscuits etc to share with your new flatmates and friends

- If you're doing any cooking at all then you'll need plates and bowels, cutlery and implements to prepare and cook food e.g. sharp knife, vegetable peeler, chopping board, wooden spoons and spatulas, large sieve, pots and pans - as well as the food itself. See the kitchen checklist at the end of this chapter for suggestions

- If a parent is taking you to university, ask if they would take you to the supermarket nearest to where you're living so you can see where it is, how it's laid out and you can buy enough food to set you up for the first week (fingers crossed: they might even contribute towards that first supermarket shop). See the useful food shopping list at the end of Chapter 5 for suggestions

- If you're in a chat with your new flatmates ahead of moving in together, you could discuss what's provided in the flat, what each of you has already and what you could buy together when you arrive. Otherwise you might end up having to store multiple kettles and toasters

- There might be a cleaning service as part of your hall package but it's likely they'll only visit once a week and only clean communal areas. You'll therefore need to wash up whatever you've used and wipe down surfaces where things have spilled on a regular basis (dull but necessary). You'll need items for cleaning e.g. sponges, washing-up liquid, surface spray, tea towels, kitchen roll

- Usually there's a broom, dustpan and brush, vacuum cleaner, mop and bucket, iron and ironing board provided (but do check)

- If you have a long-term condition such as diabetes, epilepsy or an allergy, tell your flatmates or your neighbours in your halls what your condition is and where vital medication is kept. You could keep medication and instructions in a labelled box in your kitchen cupboard - rather than in your locked room - so it's easily accessible in an emergency

Bathroom

You may have your own en suite bathroom or you may be sharing a bathroom with your flatmates.

- You'll need to provide your own towels, bath mat and toiletries

- You may or may not be responsible for cleaning the bathroom, however it will be handy to have your own cleaning items e.g. sponges and bleach

- See the bathroom checklist for suggested items to bring

Being a Good Flatmate

You'll probably be living with your flatmates for the whole of the academic year. It's unlikely you'll have the same tolerance for dirt/mess/noise so you'll have to agree what's an acceptable level you can all try to work towards.

In the Kitchen

- Clear up after yourself: wash up, dry up (replace tea towels every day or whenever dirty), put items away, wipe up spills and crumbs from surfaces, hob, fridge, floor, microwave and oven

- If the surfaces are really dirty or greasy, use kitchen roll first to soak up/ wipe off and then sponge clean

- Don't take your flatmates' stuff without asking - and replace what you borrow

- If the kitchen or recycling bins need emptying, take them out

- A cleaning rota is a good idea

In the Bathroom

- Leave it clean after using it - no-one likes a dirty, hairy bathroom

- Open a window/turn on the extractor fan whilst you're in the bathroom to let fresh air in and minimise the likelihood of mould growing

- Replace toilet rolls and put used rolls in the recycling

- Replace the hand towel every few days

- Make sure there's hand soap available

In Your Study Bedroom

- If you have your own room, you can be as untidy as you like

- But try not to be dirty: empty your bin, bring out used plates, cups etc otherwise you'll encourage bugs and your room will smell

- Your study bedrooms are usually very close to each other so you should keep your noise down e.g. music on low, if you have friends to stay then keep the sound low, close doors quietly

General House Rules

- Keep the shared areas clean and clear of your stuff

- Keep on top of any shared costs e.g. have a kitty or take it in turns for joint purchases such as toilet roll, washing up liquid, sponges

- Agree any house rules that will affect each other e.g. alcohol, smoking, drugs, noise, friends or partners staying over (whether or not, how often and for how long)

- Be nice to each other e.g. offer to make your flatmates a cup of tea or coffee, accept deliveries for them when they're out

Some Cleaning Tips

Washing Up by Hand

It's unlikely that you'll have a dishwasher in your student accommodation. Sadly, you're it.

- Scrape any food into a bin and run hot water over the items to remove any bits
    - Don't pour oil down the drain: pour it into a cup and let it harden before binning it or soak it up with a kitchen roll and then put the paper in the bin

- Run HOT water into a (clean) bowl or the sink and add a squirt of washing up liquid

- Using a sponge, wash the cleanest items first e.g. glasses and mugs
    - Ensure rims are sponged clean
    - Use non-stick sponges for non-stick pans otherwise you'll remove the non-stick coating

- Some items might need to be soaked before you can remove any burnt bits e.g. oven trays. If food is burnt into a pan or oven tray, add washing up liquid and hot water, then leave to soak for a few hours or overnight. The burnt bits should gradually lift away. Then wash as normal

- Rinse items under hot running water to check they're clean and the soap bubbles are removed

- Drying: use a clean tea towel to dry and then put away

- Wipe down the surfaces to finish

- Sweep the floor and wipe away any drips or spills for good measure

The Bathroom

- Vacuum the floor first

- Basin and shower/bath: spray areas with bathroom cleaner and, using hot water and a sponge, wipe down

- Toilet and floor: spray areas with bathroom cleaner and use kitchen roll - which you can throw away afterwards - to wipe down

- If the toilet bowl is dirty, squirt bleach around the bowl and leave it as long as you can before flushing

- Use a different colour set of washing up gloves to those you use in the kitchen

STUDY BEDROOM CHECKLIST

	Got	Packed
Pillows x 2		
Pillow cases x 4		
Duvet		
Duvet cover		
Fitted under sheet		
Mattress cover		
Mattress topper/foam		
Blanket		
Hot water bottle		
Bedside bin and bin liners		
Bedside and desk lamps (plus bulbs)		
White board/pin board and pen or pins		
Door stop		
Under-bed storage		
Room decorations e.g. photos, fairy lights, cushions, potted plant, rug		
Clothes hangers		
Wardrobe storage		

Cleaning

	Got	Packed
All-purpose cleaner		
Duster/cloths/kitchen roll		
Bin liners		

PERSONAL/HYGIENE CHECKLIST

	Got	Packed
Toothbrush		
Two pin to three pin plug adaptor for electric toothbrush		
Toothpaste		
Floss		
Brace/retainers and box		
Liquid hand soap		
Shower gel		
Shampoo & conditioner		
Cleanser		
Cotton wool		
Moisturisers - face and body		
Hair brush/comb		
Hair products & accessories		
Nail scissors and/or clippers		
Tissues: boxed and travel pack		
Deodorant		
Other face/body creams		
Razors, shaving cream, hair removal items, tweezers		
Sanitary products		
Sunscreen		
Mirror		
Contraception		
Contact lenses, case & liquid		
Make-up		
Perfume/after shave		
Prescription glasses and case		
Jewellery		
Ear buds		

FIRST AID CHECKLIST

	Got	Packed
Plasters		
Antiseptic cream		
Ibuprofen		
Paracetamol		
Decongestant		
Antihistamine – for allergies/bug bites/stings		
Milk of Magnesia liquid for times of excess		
Specific personal medication		

OTHER USEFUL STUFF CHECKLIST

	Got	Packed
Hobby/interest e.g. books, computer games, consoles		
Playing cards or other games		
Small sewing kit with needles and a variety of threads		
Lunch box		
Water bottle		
Thermos flask (wide neck – can also use for hot lunches e.g. pasta/rice)		
Torch		
Musical instrument		
Address book		
Bicycle and kit		
Sports kit and bag		
Umbrella		
Sleeping bag		
Dressing up/fancy dress clothes		
Single white flat sheet (for toga) plus belt and safety pins		
Sports clothes		
Swimming costume, goggles and towel		
Flip flops (for showers/ communal areas)		
First term: winter clothes		
Formal/evening wear		

KITCHEN CHECKLIST

	Got	Packed
Plates - large and small x 2 of each		
Bowls x 2		
Set of cheap cutlery – pieces often go missing		
Drinking glasses x 2		
Mugs x 2		
Pack of disposable cups for visitors		
Pans: frying pan, small and large saucepans with lids		
Oven tray – a small, deep tray can double up as a cake tin		
Chopping knives x 2		
Chopping board		
Tin opener		
Bottle opener		
Wooden spoons/spatulas		
Kettle		
Toaster		
Potato/vegetable peeler		
Large sieve		
Potato masher		
Cheese grater		
Jug		
Clingfilm		
Foil		
Weighing scales		
Small sealable plastic bags		
Plastic boxes with lids for storage		
Fruit bowl/mixing bowl		
Bag closers		
Kitchen scissors (easier than a knife for cutting up meat)		
Casserole/pie dish		
Oven gloves		
Hand-held blender e.g. for smoothies		

	Got	Packed
Washing up liquid		
Kitchen surface spray		
Washing up gloves		
Scrubbing sponges for washing up		
Flat sponges for wiping surfaces		
Tea towels		
Kitchen roll – lots		
Bin liners		

BATHROOM CHECKLIST

	Got	Packed
Bath towels x 2		
Hand towels x 3		
Bath mat		
Hanging shower basket		
Cleaning:		
Bathroom spray cleaner		
Bleach		
Bathroom cleaning sponges (for the basin, bath/shower)		
Kitchen roll (for cleaning the toilet and floor)		
Washing up gloves (separate to the kitchen pair)		
Toilet rolls		
Mould and mildew remover spray		

4

Laundry

It's likely you'll make some mistakes when doing your laundry and some items will change colour, lose their shape or shrink. Hopefully, most of that can be avoided by following the advice below.

This advice is a general guide to laundry. You must check the labels of your laundry in case some items require special handling e.g. hand wash only, dry clean only.

Frequency

- Whenever dirty/smelly!

- After one use: underwear, T-shirts, sports wear

- After a few wears/uses: pyjamas, outer clothes, pillow cases, towels

- Weekly/fortnightly: bedding

Temperature

- Towels and sheets normally 60°C

- Most other items normally 40°C

- Some items will need to be washed at a delicate 30°C e.g. fine tops or woollen jumpers. You probably won't have many of these so you might want to share a delicate machine wash with a friend or just wash by hand

Cost & Paying for Laundry

Laundry costs add up. A load of washing can be £2.80 and using the dryer £1.40 = £4.20 per load.

- The machines in halls are usually industrial size so you can launder a bin-bag size amount in one go

- When not washing towels or bedding, you might not have much laundry so consider sharing a load - and the cost - with a friend or flatmate

- Some people use specially designed sheets that you add to a mixed load of laundry: they stop colour runs by absorbing dye particles from the wash water. This could save you money by allowing you to do mixed colour loads. Read the instructions before using

- To save money, you could avoid the drying cost and, instead, invest in a clothes horse/airer. Some halls have drying rooms

Many university launderettes use cashless systems

- If it's cashless, there may be an app and/or a reloadable card that you purchase from the university reception, launderette or retail outlet on the campus

- A laundry app might identify when your laundry cycle is finished, which machines are free or when the launderette is at its quietest

How to...

Sort Your Laundry

- Separate your laundry according to colour and wash temperature

- Shake out clothes e.g. straighten sleeves and trouser legs, un-ball socks

- Empty pockets

- Wash jeans and sweaters inside out

- Wash clothes with transfers/vinyl decoration inside out and don't tumble them

- Do up zips and buttons before washing so that clothes keep their shape

- Check symbols for washing instructions

- Put tiny items e.g. G-strings or footsies into a mesh bag for washing. Plumbers can charge around £40 to clear a blockage where something small has slipped down inside the washing machine drum

Use a Washing Machine

- Have the correct coins/loaded laundry card/laundry app on your phone

- Before putting clothes in, spin the drum (where the clothes go) by hand and look inside to check no clothes have been left behind e.g. a stray sock. Otherwise they could discolour your laundry

- Check that items can be washed in a washing machine - check the washing symbol on the label

- Put clothes in one item at a time so they are loosely piled in the machine

- Leave a gap of at least 10cm (a fist) at the top. If you overfill the machine then the clothes won't be cleaned properly

- Add the detergent: read the recommended amount and either add to the detergent drawer (middle section or labelled II) or put in the dispenser ball and place on the top of the laundry and towards the back of the machine
  - Check what type of detergent is used at home. Non-bio might be a better option if you have sensitive skin e.g. eczema

- Shut the door firmly and select the correct setting - usually by temperature or fabric

- Check the machine has started - it might not start if the door hasn't shut properly

- Check the time to complete the wash on the display and return a few minutes before this time

- You could leave your clothes basket in front or on top of the machine so, if you're late back, the next person has somewhere to put your clean laundry

- If the door doesn't open immediately on finishing, wait 1-2 minutes and try again - some machines have that safety feature built in

- Take the clothes out and spin the drum by hand/check inside to make sure you've not left anything behind

Hand Wash

A few items might require hand-washing. Hopefully not too many.

- Dissolve detergent in warm (not hot) water

- Wearing washing up gloves, dunk the item(s) and let them soak in the water for a few minutes so the detergent can get to work. Gently knead the items especially those areas that touch the body most often or are obviously soiled

- Gently squeeze out the water from the item(s), let the dirty water drain away

- Rinse in clean, cool water three times

- You may need to wrap the item(s) in a clean towel to help remove the excess water and then shake out and lay flat to dry

Use a Tumble Dryer

- Have the correct coins/loaded laundry card/laundry app on your phone

- Always remove fluff from the tumble dryer filter before and after you've used the machine

- If it's a condenser dryer, pour away the collected water from the container before and after using

- Check that items can be tumbled - look for the drying symbol: a circle inside a square

- Shake clothes out before putting in the dryer

- You may want to use two dryers for two separate loads: one for smaller items such as underwear (not bras - don't tumble these), pyjamas, lightweight tops etc which take less time to dry, and another for bedding, towels and heavy items such as hoodies, which will take longer

- Shut the door firmly and select the correct setting - usually by temperature or time

- Check the machine has started - it might not start if the door hasn't shut properly
  - Check the time to complete the dry on the display and return a few minutes before this time
  - You could leave your clothes basket in front or on top of the machine so, if you're late back, the next person has somewhere to put your dry laundry
  - At the end, check the machine is empty - look inside the drum

Iron

- Check the care symbol on the item's label to ensure it can be ironed and at what heat

- Turn the dial to the correct temperature and wait for the iron to heat up

- Lay the item on the ironing board and adjust it so it's flat
  - Where the material is layered, e.g. trousers or sleeves, ensure the material underneath is also flat

- Avoid ironing over buttons, zips, hems and seams

- You can reduce the likelihood of wrinkling - and therefore ironing - by:
  - Not overstuffing the washing machine
  - Taking your clothes out of the washing machine as soon as it's finished

- Shaking out your clothes and lying them flat on a clothes horse or on hangers to dry
- When they're dry, fold them away or hang them on clothes hangers

LAUNDRY CHECKLIST

	Got	Packed
Laundry detergent		
Laundry basket		
Small mesh bag for tinies		
Clothes horse/airer		
Radiator airer		
Laundry bag		

Key to Common Laundry Symbols

Wash . . . .

**Wash at or
below 40°C**

Hand wash

Do not wash

Number inside the symbol = maximum wash temperature
Horizontal bars under the symbol: None = cotton = maximum wash and spin
One bar = synthetic = medium wash and spin
Two bars = silk or wool = delicate wash and spin

Dry . . . .

**Tumble drying
(low temperature)**

**Tumble drying
(normal)**

**Do not
tumble dry**

Line dry

Dry flat

Drip dry

Iron ·

**Iron at low
temperature**

**Iron at medium
temperature**

**Iron at high
temperature**

Do not iron

Professional Cleaning ·

**Professional
cleaning symbol**

**Do not
dry clean**

Letters inside the circle and horizontal lines
under the symbol are instructions for the
professional cleaner

5

Food & Drink

Try to eat and drink healthily: you'll look and feel better for it.

Amongst other things, what you eat and drink affects your body shape, skin, eyes, hair and teeth; your mood, energy levels and ability to study and socialise; your digestive system, your heart and other organs; your strength, stamina and bone density; your sleep; your immune system; and your body's ability to grow and repair itself. So it's pretty important to eat the right food and in the correct amounts.

What Constitutes a Healthy Diet?

Unless you have specific dietary requirements, a healthy diet should include the following food groups. The majority of this information is taken from the NHS Eat Well guidelines.

- Carbohydrates - one third of what you eat each day
    - E.g. potatoes (skins on), brown or wholegrain bread, brown rice, wholewheat pasta, low sugar cereal

- Choose wholegrain, higher fibre and low sugar options
- Carbs give you energy, they contain fibre (important for your digestive system), they contain vitamins and minerals, and they make you feel full

- Protein
  - Including meat, fish, eggs, pulses, nuts
  - Pulses - such as beans, peas and lentils - are a good alternative to meat because they're lower in fat, higher in fibre and protein, and cost less than meat
  - Government guidelines are to have two portions of fish each week, one of which should be oily e.g. salmon or mackerel
  - If eating meat, choose lean cuts, take the skin off poultry and eat less red and processed meat such as bacon, ham and sausages
  - Protein is essential to grow and repair cells, contains vitamins and minerals and helps you stay fuller for longer

- Vegetables and fruit - make them just over a third of what you eat per day
  - Eat a variety and at least five portions per day
  - Fresh, frozen, tinned, dried or juiced are all good
  - Juice and/or smoothies are high in sugar and should be limited to 150ml a day
  - Vegetables and fruit provide important vitamins and minerals to help your body work properly and stay healthy
  - They're also an excellent source of fibre and can help prevent constipation and other digestive problems

- Dairy/dairy alternatives
  - You could add it throughout the day e.g. milk with cereal, tea and coffee; butter or spread on sandwiches or toast; yoghurt or cheese for dessert
  - Choose lower fat and lower sugar versions
  - Dairy and dairy alternatives are a great source of protein, some vitamins, calcium and help keep bones strong

- Oil
  - Choose unsaturated oils and spreads in small quantities e.g. vegetable, olive, sunflower and rapeseed oil
  - Fats help the body absorb vitamins A, D and E, which contribute to healthy eyes, skin, bones and the immune system

- Drink 6 to 8 cups/glasses of fluid a day
  - Water quenches your thirst, it's free and it's good for you
  - Unsweetened tea, fruit tea, coffee, semi-skimmed, 1% fat or skimmed milk are also healthy alternatives
  - If you don't drink enough fluid, you might find it difficult to concentrate or think clearly or you may become constipated

If you want to eat or drink something sugary, fatty or salty, have these foodstuffs less often and in small amounts.

Spoon Sizes in Recipes

Tsp = tsp = 5ml = 1 x tea spoon
Dsp = dessert spoon = 10ml = 2 x tea spoons
Tbsp = table spoon = 15ml = 3 x tea spoons

Cooking - Some General Advice

- Get your parents or friends to show you how to make dishes you like and that are healthy, quick and easy to prepare

- Make a meal several portions in size then you can have the second portion at a later date, which will save you from having to cook from scratch again, or you can share with a friend

- Offer to buy, prepare, cook and clear away a meal for friend or flatmate once a week and get them to do the same for you = one less meal to organise

- Instead of ordering a take-away - which is usually expensive and high in fat, salt and sugar - use a good quality, low sugar and low salt variety of pasta sauce, curry sauce or pesto as a speedy base for dishes

- It's really important for health to eat colourful (not just beige) food

- Ideally have two different vegetables with every meal - you'll quickly get your 5 a day

- If cooking your veg on the hob, use a small amount of water to just cover the vegetables. Stir at least once and don't boil the life out of them. Usually takes 5-7 minutes

- After touching raw fish or meat, wash your hands with soap and hot water and wash any chopping board or utensils with hot water and washing up liquid

- Follow the cooking instructions on packaging

- Set the timer on your oven/phone in case you get distracted and forget you're cooking

- Do you know how to serve everything hot at the same time? Keeping it covered means it will stay hot for around 5-10 minutes. If you've boiled food, pour away the water so it doesn't continue to cook and put the lid back on the pan. Or put hot food on a warm plate then cover with foil

Storing Leftovers

Keep any untouched (never half eaten: this is full of bacteria) leftovers - they can be a welcome quick and easy next meal.

- Cool down leftovers as quickly as possible (in 1-2 hours) then put into a container, cover and put in the fridge or freezer

- Cover your food securely. It stops anything from the shelf above dropping onto it, it will prevent the food from drying out and, if the container is tilted or pushed over, the contents are less likely to spill

- Always empty food out of metal tins into plastic storage pots/bags

- Eat leftovers from the fridge within 1-2 days

- If food is re-heated, always make sure it's piping hot before serving

- Rice must be cooled within 1 hour, stored in the fridge, eaten within a day, re-heated only once and must be steaming hot all the way through before serving

Five Easy Meals

Each of these simple recipes makes two portions: one to eat and one to share or save. Check cooking times on packaging and adjust accordingly. Stir all pans at least once during cooking.

Spaghetti Bolognese with Salad

1. Boil a pan of water and add two portions of spaghetti. Prepare a salad
2. Pan fry 200g of minced beef until brown (this is important for flavour). When browned, pour any excess oil into a mug (when cooled, soak up with kitchen roll and throw away)
3. Optional: If you want extra flavour/bulk you could add chopped carrots, mushrooms, bacon, lentils (pre-cooked from a tin or packet for speed), garlic, herbs (e.g. oregano, basil), a squirt of ketchup or tomato puree, a stock cube, a bit of wine (any type)
4. Add half a jar of pasta sauce to the meat and heat through; simmer for 15 minutes
5. Drain the pasta and grate some cheese
6. Serve the Bolognese with grated cheese, pasta and salad

You can transform the Bolognese - or the spare portion - into a Chilli con Carne by reheating with a small tin of spicy beans and serving with a dollop of cream cheese or crème fraiche or sour cream

Chicken Korma with Rice, Broccoli, Green Beans and Naan Bread

1. Boil a pan of water and add two portions of rice
2. Slice two breasts of chicken. Heat 1 teaspoon of oil in a frying pain and, when hot, add the chicken. Turn down the heat to medium and pan fry until lightly browned and no longer pink in the middle
3. Boil a second pan of water and add broccoli and green beans
4. Add half a jar of korma sauce to the chicken and heat through
5. If you want extra flavour/bulk you could add a small tin of butter beans, some cashew nuts or a handful of raisins and heat through
6. Drain the rice, broccoli and green beans and lightly toast the naan bread
7. Serve the chicken korma with the rice, broccoli, green beans and naan bread

Pesto Pasta with Chicken, Peas and Sweetcorn

1. Boil a pan of water and add two portions of pasta
2. Slice two breasts of chicken. Heat 1 teaspoon of oil in a frying pain and, when hot, add the chicken. Turn down the heat to medium and pan fry until lightly browned and no longer pink in the middle
3. Add frozen peas and sweetcorn to the pasta and cook for 3-4 minutes
4. Drain the pasta, peas and sweetcorn, add the cooked chicken and two dessert spoons of pesto, stir through and serve

Pan Fried Salmon Fillet with Potatoes, Green Beans and Spinach

1. Boil a pan of water and add two portions of halved new potatoes
2. Wait 5 minutes then boil a second pan of water and, to this pan, add the green beans and spinach

3. Heat 1 teaspoon of oil in a frying pain and, when hot, add the salmon. Turn down the heat to medium, sprinkle a little salt and pepper over the fish and pan fry until it's cooked all the way through
4. Add 2 teaspoons of butter and 1 teaspoon of lemon juice to the pan and heat through
5. Drain the new potatoes, green beans and spinach and serve the salmon, butter and lemon sauce

Roasted Potatoes and Vegetables Topped with Crumbled Goats Cheese

1. Heat the oven to 180°C fan/200°C regular oven
2. In a bowl, make a marinade of 2 tablespoons of olive oil, 1 teaspoon of grainy mustard, 1 tablespoon of runny honey and salt and pepper
3. Wash and chop two sweet potatoes into the size of new potatoes or halve 10 new potatoes and put in a large oven tray (or do a mix of both). Add a selection of vegetables chopped into large pieces e.g. peppers, courgette, aubergine, red onion, mushrooms, carrots, butternut squash, whole baby tomatoes, baby corn
4. Stir the marinade and pour over the vegetables; stir to ensure the vegetables are coated
5. Roast the vegetables in the middle of the oven (stirring half way) for about 30 minutes until the potatoes are soft
6. Serve the roasted vegetables with some goat's cheese crumbled on top and sliced French bread on the side

Light Meal/Snack Ideas

Stuck for ideas? Try one of these:

- Toast/crumpets/bagels/sandwiches/wraps/pitta/crackers/rice cakes with:
    - Cheese and tomato, tuna mayo with sweetcorn or cucumber, salad and hummus, mashed avocado, cooked chicken and salad, scrambled egg, brie and cranberry, peanut butter, egg mayonnaise, smoked salmon and cream cheese

- Jacket potato with:
    - Curried chicken, grated cheese and baked beans, chilli, roasted vegetables, tuna mayo with sweetcorn

- Fruit: fresh, dried, tinned, frozen or juiced

- Soup and a sandwich

- Cereal with fruit, nuts and/or seeds and milk

- Yoghurt - add fruit and muesli to make it more filling

USEFUL SHOPPING LIST

PRODUCE		
Fruit		
Vegetables - frozen might last longer/be more economical		
Salad		
BAKERY		
E.g. bread/bagels/pitta/naan - most can be frozen if you have too much		
PACKETS/JARS/TINS/BOXES		
Rice/pasta/noodles		
Stir-in sauces for pasta/curry/stir fry		
Sauces e.g. soy, vinegar, ketchup, sweet chili, mayonnaise, tomato puree		
Tinned tuna/other fish		
Tinned vegetables e.g. tomatoes, baked beans, lentils, beans, chickpeas		
Seasoning e.g. salt & pepper, stock cubes		
Dried herbs and spices e.g. basil, oregano, chilli, turmeric, curry, cumin		
Oil for cooking/dressings		
Breakfast cereal		
Eggs		
Toast/sandwich fillings e.g. jam, honey, Marmite, peanut butter		
Snacks to share e.g. biscuits, crisps, nuts, popcorn, chocolate		
Sugar		
DAIRY/CHILLED		
Milk/dairy alternative		
Butter/spread		
Cheese		
Yoghurt		
Hummus/other dips		
Meat/other e.g. chicken, mince (buy the best you can afford), fish, Quorn		
Pizza/ready meals - frozen is often cheaper		
DRINKS		
Tea, coffee, hot chocolate		
Fruit juice		
Alcohol/non-alcoholic drink to celebrate & mixers		

"Don't stress about anything before you get there - remember everyone arrives in exactly the same boat"

(Male, age 20)

6

Friendships & Relationships

Friendships

Many of you will have attended the same school or college for the last seven years: you know who everyone is and you know all their stories. Going to university's an opportunity to meet a bunch of new people. Most of them are likely to be around your age and many of them will have a similar outlook or interests to you.

One of the Best Things about Being at University

In my research, meeting new people and making new friends was considered to be one of the best things about being at university. Plus, if you're living away from home, you're able to spend as much time with these new friends as you like:

"Meeting loads of new people and the whole social experience of being around friends all the time"
(Male, age 19)

"All of the new people you meet and constantly being surrounded by and living with friends"
(Female, age 18)

"Meeting new people from completely different places who you wouldn't normally be friends with"
(Female, age 18)

Finding and Making New Friends

It's common for new students to feel some anxiety about finding and making new friends but try not to worry.

If you're feeling vulnerable, awkward or shy, just remember that most students tend to arrive at the same time, many of them won't know anyone else either, they're probably feeling the same way as you and most will want to make friends.

There are lots of opportunities to meet people:

- Even before you arrive, you can start the process
  - Most universities have moderated social media accounts for new students
  - Once your place is confirmed, log on and find your university hall, block, corridor or flatmates, your course, or clubs and societies you're interested in joining
  - Don't be shy: join in. It'll make the first day so much better to know names, faces and a bit about people ahead of time
  - It's also a good way to keep up-to-date with Freshers' events

- If you're living away from home, your flatmates are likely to be the first people you meet
  - You might have a shared kitchen or lounge: if you hear people are in it, take a deep breath, put on a big smile and go and say hello

- Take a door stop to prop your door open when you're in - it shows you're welcoming. And keep a packet of biscuits in your room to share with anyone who drops by

- You'll see the people on your course regularly and you already have a subject interest in common
  - If you're on a course where there are hundreds of other people in your lectures then it might feel difficult to talk to anyone. But we're creatures of habit and we often sit in the same place so you're likely to start recognising the same faces. Smile and say hello
  - Seminars and tutorials should start in weeks 2 or 3. You'll be in smaller groups and you'll start to recognise the same people each week, which will make it easier to talk to each other

- Join societies and clubs that you have a genuine interest in
  - This is a great way to make friends as you have common interests, which gives you something to talk about/do together
  - If you're focused on something, you're less likely to experience awkward silences

- You're likely to be in many, many queues - from getting your room key to lining up for food, standing at a bar to waiting outside a classroom. Smile and say hello to the person standing next to you

Talking to everyone and being open to making friends was a recurring piece of advice from the first year students in my research:

"Don't worry too much about which friendships will last and which ones won't. Try to meet as many people as possible and it will soon settle"
(Male, age 20)

"Introduce yourself to everyone you meet or sit next to in lectures because you never know who might turn out to be your good friends"
(Female, age 18)

"Chat to anyone and everyone you can in the first few weeks – this is how you'll make most of your friends! Don't be shy"
(Female, age 18)

"Take every opportunity to make friends and go out, especially during Freshers' Week, even if you're tired!"
(Female, age 18)

And there are lots of things you can do to help smooth things along, for example:

- Topics of conversation - you can initiate it: where they're from, what they're studying, where they're living, what clubs or societies they're joining or interests they have, the weather

- Offer to make your flatmates a cup of tea or coffee, or go for tea and coffee during breaks in classes with your course mates

- Offer to walk together e.g. to class, to a club, to the library or to a bar

- And smile at people. When we're nervous or anxious we often look away too quickly after smiling at people in case they don't return a smile. Wait a second longer before you turn away since they might not have been expecting to see a friendly face

Freshers' Week

The first week you arrive at university is generally known as Freshers' (or Welcome) Week. This is the time when the Students' Union puts on social, academic, sporting and interest events.

- Do attend different events and society meetings that appeal to you: it's a great way to try out new activities or continue with interests you already have

- You don't have to commit to a club straight away - you can normally attend a trial session

- Don't feel under pressure to go to clubs and bars and drink alcohol during Freshers' Week if that's not your thing
    - There are an increasing number of fun 'Sober Socials' - events that don't involve alcohol and nightclubs - in response to a growing number of students wanting to attend alcohol-free get-togethers

- Societies and clubs are a great way to meet people since their members have similar interests to you. The students in my research were keen to recommend this

"Join at least one society or sport"
(Male, age 19)

"Find friends that are of a similar mindset through joining societies of things you love/enjoy."
(Female, age 18)

Don't Panic

- The first few weeks at university aren't the only time you'll get to meet people, so don't worry if you don't find your close friends straightaway. The first year students in my research were keen to emphasise this - and that you will find your friends:

"Don't worry…there's thousands of people there so if you don't click with people straight away, give it time"
(Male, age 19)

"Don't stress about making friends straight away, it happens eventually"
(Male, age 18)

"Don't expect to make friends for life in the first week – it takes time to find people similar to you"
(Female, age 19)

- Also, you don't have to stay attached to the first friendly person you bump into - unless you want to
  - Although some great friendships can be made in the first few weeks, you'll be meeting new and interesting people throughout your entire time at university e.g. through societies, taking different course modules, through other people

"Talk to lots of people on your course or join clubs/societies to meet new people and don't feel like you have to be best friends with the first people you meet"
(Female, age 18)

- If you're feeling a bit lonely, sad or homesick, read Chapter 9
  - You'll see that you're not alone and, for most students, over time you'll become more settled and things will get better

- And, from the research that I undertook, this is my favourite quote:

"There will be people who like you, always"
(Female, age 19)

I Know We've Only Just Met But Shall We Live Together?

It's becoming increasingly common for first year students to organise accommodation for their second year in the first term of their first year.

- This means that you might find yourself committing to living with people - in a year's time and for an academic year - who you've only known for just over a month!

- You can choose to do this or not. You just need to weigh up whether you feel more comfortable having this organised ahead of time - even if it means that your flatmates might not turn out to be your close friends - or whether you'd be happy to let things develop more slowly and naturally over time

- It might be reassuring to know:
    - Student accommodation is often located in neighbouring areas so you'll probably be living near your close friends even if you don't live with them
    - Sometimes you can really like someone but find them impossible to live with so it's not always best to live with your friends
    - When you share a home you get to know people well so you might develop unexpected friendships with your new housemates

- It's also worth bearing in mind that committing to your second year's accommodation early on means you'll need to pay a month's deposit within weeks of handing over your first year's deposit. Given the cost of accommodation you might need to be able to access somewhere in the region of £500-1,000, which will be tied up in your first and second years' accommodation deposits

- You should also be aware that, if it's student housing you're renting, it's common practice to take over the tenancy from the date the current students vacate the property. So, even if you're not moving in until September/October, you may be paying rent and bills from July

- Check with your university accommodation department since they might offer a range of services on aspects of private sector tenancy, such as a contract-checking service and advice on housing regulations

- And, if you choose not to commit in that first month of starting university, really don't worry. You'll still find somewhere to live and people to live with in a year's time. For example:

- It's not uncommon for friendships or circumstances to change over the course of a year and someone who committed early on to a house might decide against it at a later date - leaving a room needing to be filled
- You may find that, if available, living in a hall of residence suits you in your second year

And you may not have to move out of university accommodation at all. Students at some, particularly collegiate, universities may be able to stay living in their college accommodation for a further year or two.

Relationships, Sex & Intimacy

(Did the book fall open at this page?)

There are likely to be thousands of people, many the same age as you, at your university. Amongst all of those people, it's likely there will be some who you're attracted to.

Just like you, they're bright, they're excited to be there, they're keen to meet other people, many of them will have the same interests and outlook as you, lots of them are living away from home for the first time and they're experiencing complete freedom to do what they like and date whoever they fancy. With all that power comes responsibility.

Questions to Ask Yourself

Prior to embarking on any intimacy, ask yourself:

- Would you still fancy that person in the cold light of day?
  - Would it be awkward or lovely to see them again?

- Would you still be their cup of tea tomorrow? You'll have an idea of this if you know them already

- Do they treat you well every time you see them? Are they excited to see you? Do they introduce you to their friends?

- Do you feel you're being pressured into intimacy or having sex? Perhaps to keep your partner or to impress other people?
  - Don't ever feel pressured into any form of intimacy or having sex

- Are you putting pressure on someone to be intimate with you?
  - If you're struggling with the issue of consent just imagine that, instead of initiating sex, you're making someone a cup of tea. Take a look at this excellent video, 'Tea Consent', which explains what consent is when it comes to sexual interactions: https://youtu.be/oQbei5JGiT8

And remember that:

- Intimacy and sex are expressions of love and you or your partner might wish to wait a significant period of time or until a long term commitment has been made

- Intimacy and sex aren't the only aspects of a relationship, and there are other ways of enjoying each other's company

Advice on Intimacy

If you decide to be intimate with someone:

- Prior to entering into a sexual relationship, consider being tested for STIs (sexually transmitted infections)

- If you have sex with a man, use a condom. Condoms help reduce the spread of STIs. These infections include HIV (Human Immunodeficiency Virus), chlamydia, genital herpes, genital warts, gonorrhoea, hepatitis B, and syphilis

- If you're in a male/female couple, in addition to a condom you should use another form of contraception to prevent an unintended pregnancy

- If you're certain that you want to be intimate with someone: be respectful, be clean, be kind, use contraception and be enthusiastic!

- If you've had unprotected sex or your contraception fails:
    - Emergency contraception can prevent pregnancy
    - There are currently two types of emergency contraception: the emergency contraceptive pill (the 'morning after' pill) and the intrauterine device (IUD or coil)
    - Don't delay in seeking emergency contraception, the sooner you use it, the more effective it will be
    - You can get emergency contraception for free from a variety of centres including GP surgeries, contraception clinics and some pharmacies (and some of those pharmacies can be found in supermarkets), but they may not all fit the IUD

- If you regret being intimate with someone:
    - Don't be too hard on yourself. We all make mistakes and the thing to do is learn from those mistakes and move on a little wiser
    - Put it down to experience, acknowledge you've learned a lesson and try not to let it happen again

Existing Relationships

Perhaps you're already in a relationship with someone. If you're moving away then it might feel very hard to leave them.

- Do throw yourself into university life: go to Freshers' Week and make friends, join clubs and societies, meet your flatmates and find the people on your course. These are the people who you'll be with on a day-to-day basis - some for the next three to four years - and they often end up being friends for life

- It might feel a bit hard to keep a relationship going when there's so much going on in your new life - but it's certainly possible

- If your partner has also gone to university then that could be helpful as you'll have an understanding of each other's daily lives and can share experiences

- If your partner hasn't gone to university, then they might find it difficult to imagine your new life and might even feel a bit threatened by you striking out on your own and how busy and exciting your new life appears to be

- Invite them to visit and keep speaking and texting so they feel involved and can picture you in, and continue to be part of, your new life

There's over £150m in scholarships available to UK students each year.... Organisations often struggle to attract enough applicants - therefore your chances of being successful if you apply are greater than you might think.

(The Scholarship Hub)

7

Money: Where It Goes & How To Get More Of It

One of the most important things you learn as a student is how to budget and how to live on a restricted income. Not having enough money, however, is a common complaint - and worry - amongst students.

Where It Goes

Assuming you know how much money you'll have at the beginning of each term then you need to allocate your money to the following areas:

- Rent: this is likely to be your biggest outgoing

- Utility bills e.g. gas, electricity, water, phone/broadband. These may be included if you're in halls or in some rental properties but you must check and allocate your money accordingly

- Insurance: even if you're in a hall your gadgets might only be insured within your room but not outside, so you may need additional cover

- Mobile phone: If you're out of contract and you're happy with your phone, there are some great SIM only deals available

- Anything course-related e.g. books, kit, equipment, uniform, printing, membership, field trips

- Travel: to university/work/going out/going home. Usually by public transport but may include the occasional taxi. Discount rail and coach cards are a good idea but they usually need to be renewed annually

- Food and personal items. Include medical items such as contact lenses

- Socialising e.g. coffees, soft drinks, snacks, alcohol, entry into nightclubs, cinema, gigs

- Club/societies e.g. memberships, subs, equipment, kit, travel, entry into pool, gym etc

- Clothes and shoes

- Extras – there are ALWAYS extras or unexpected items

BUDGET TABLE

	Amount per TERM (£)
Rent	
Utility bills	
Insurance	
Mobile phone	
Course-related costs	
Travel	
Food and personal items	
Socialising	
Club/societies	
Clothes and shoes	
Extras	
TOTAL	£
Total amount of money you have at the start of each TERM	£
Minus Total above	£
Leaves you with...	£

Rent

If you're living away from home, rent is usually your biggest expenditure.

- Save the Student, the student money website for everything student finance, carries out an annual National Student Money Survey. It has some particularly useful tables on its website that show average student living costs and also average rent at each university around the country. Take a look at this link for information:
  - https://www.savethestudent.org/money/student-budgeting/what-do-students-spend-their-money-on.html

Accommodation deposits

If you're living away from home, a very large additional item is your accommodation deposit: it could be one month's rent.

- It's becoming increasingly common for students to organise their accommodation for their second year in the first term of their first year. This means that, within a matter of weeks of paying up to a month's deposit for your first year's accommodation, you could be paying another month's deposit for your second year's accommodation

- Realistically, given the cost of accommodation, you may need to be able to access somewhere in the region of £500-1,000, which will be tied up in the two deposits

Healthcare Costs

If you're a UK resident then you're probably used to most medical treatment being free (at the point of delivery) under the NHS.

When you become 19, however, if you're registered with a GP in England, you'll normally have to start paying for some elements of your healthcare e.g. prescriptions, which are currently charged at £9.

There are ways that you might be able to reduce these costs:

- If your savings, investments or property don't exceed £16,000 (including your maintenance loan, parental contribution and part-time work) then you might qualify for free or discounted medical costs under the NHS Low Income Scheme
    - You'll need to fill in the NHS HC1 form, which you can find here:
    - https://www.nhsbsa.nhs.uk/nhs-low-income-scheme

- If you're over the financial threshold and you need regular prescriptions you can pay a set price for prescriptions for 3 or 12 months, no matter how many you need
    - You can find further information about the NHS Prescription Prepayment Certificate here:
    - https://apps.nhsbsa.nhs.uk/ppc-online/patient.do

If you're registered with a GP in Scotland, Wales or Northern Ireland then prescriptions are currently free.

Tuition Fees

Students from England, Scotland, Wales, Northern Ireland and EU countries can apply for tuition fee loans from the UK student finance organisations.

- If you're eligible, these loans are paid directly to the university from the student finance company (therefore you won't need to allocate money for tuition in your termly budget)

- Tuition fees in the UK are set by the university and are currently up to £9,250 per year of full-time undergraduate study

- The value of the tuition fee loan varies depending on factors such as:
  - Whether the course is full- or part-time
  - Whether you're attending a public or private university
  - Where in the UK the university is located
  - Where you're from
  - Whether you're on a placement year e.g. on an industrial placement or studying abroad

- If you're studying an accelerated degree course, the tuition fee loan could be up to £11,100 per year to account for the additional tuition delivered across a shorter time period (see p98 for more information)

- If you live in Scotland, or an EU country, and decide to study at a university in Scotland, you currently won't have to pay anything towards tuition fees (criteria apply)

You should check with the student finance organisations directly for eligibility criteria and details of the loan. See p89 for the list of UK student finance organisations.

How to Support Yourself Whilst Studying

Maintenance Loan

If you're from the UK, you can apply to the government for a maintenance loan to go towards living costs.

- How much maintenance loan you get depends on various factors e.g. where you're from, where you're studying, your household income, whether you're living at home or not, whether you're studying full- or part-time, if you're over 60

- Maintenance loans are paid directly into your bank account, in three instalments, usually at the start of each term (monthly if studying in Scotland)

The table below shows the maintenance loan for full-time students from England for the academic year 2019/20.

Full-time student	2019 to 2020
Living at home	Up to £7,529
Living away from home, outside London	Up to £8,944
Living away from home, in London	Up to £11,672
Student spends a year of a UK course studying abroad	Up to £10,242

Source: https://www.gov.uk/student-finance/new-fulltime-students

Follow this link for a handy student finance calculator for students from England or the EU starting a new undergraduate course:

- www.gov.uk/student-finance-calculator

- It estimates student loans and extra state funding e.g. if you're disabled or have children. Your result will be more accurate if you know your annual household income (your parents' or partner's income plus your own)

Follow these links for information on student loans in the respective countries:

- England: www.gov.uk/student-finance

- Scotland: www.saas.gov.uk

- Wales: www.studentfinancewales.co.uk

- Northern Ireland: www.studentfinanceni.co.uk

The amount of maintenance loan you receive may not be sufficient to even pay your rent. You must therefore find other ways to make ends meet

Government Grants/Allowances

You may be eligible for additional financial support in the form of government grants or allowances, which you can apply for when you apply for student loans.

- They're available to meet a range of needs, for example if you:
  - Have a disability, long-term health condition, mental health condition or specific learning difficulty (such as dyslexia)
  - Are a medical or social worker, or teacher training student
  - Have been in local authority care
  - Are estranged from your parents
  - Are a student with children
  - Have adults who depend on you
  - Are on a low income
  - Are studying abroad - you might get a grant to cover some travel expenses

Your Family

Your family - possibly parents or grandparents - may be in a position to support you in some way.

- You should discuss this with them in advance so you know whether and how much money they're able to give you and how often you'll receive that money. You may find budgeting easier if you receive money on a weekly basis

- The amount you receive in the maintenance loan is partly based on family income therefore this does imply that your parents are expected to help you financially, where they're able

- As a guide, you could ask your parents to make up the shortfall between the maintenance loan you receive and the maximum maintenance loan. For example, if you're an undergraduate student studying full-time from England:
    - The maximum maintenance loan in 2019/20 for a student living away from home, outside London is £8,944
    - If you receive £6,944 in maintenance loan then you could ask your parents to contribute £2,000 per year towards your living costs

- If they're able to contribute more this would be helpful since many students find it difficult to live on this level of income

- It's possible, however, that your family isn't able to contribute towards your living costs

Savings

Try and build up your savings, e.g. from part-time jobs and gifts, before you leave for university so you have money to fall back on whilst you're waiting for your next instalment of funding.

Scholarships, Bursaries, Grants & Awards

According to The Scholarship Hub, which helps students find alternative sources of funding, there's over £150m in scholarships available to UK students each year. It also states that organisations often struggle to attract enough applicants - therefore your chances of being successful if you apply are greater than you might think.

There are a number of useful resources where you can search for funding to see whether you qualify, how much you could get and how to apply.

- Universities
    - Websites: search under scholarships, grants, awards and bursaries
    - At open days: attend the finance talk to hear what they have to say about alternative sources of funding
    - Student finance department: talk to them directly as they might know of pots of money that haven't yet been listed on the university website

- Useful websites that have assembled the details of a huge number of trusts, foundations, etc include:
    - The Scholarship Hub: www.thescholarshiphub.org.uk
    - Turn2us is a national charity that helps people in financial hardship gain access to welfare benefits, charitable grants and support services www.turn2us.org.uk

- Look in your school/university/careers library for the book 'The Guide to Educational Grants'

- The time to apply varies - don't panic if you've already started a course
    - Some organisations invite applications whilst you're studying for A levels or when you have your university place confirmed, some stipulate that you should be in your first or subsequent years, and others are only available on graduation

- Start looking early so you can identify deadlines and have sufficient time to gather your evidence and prepare your application

- Unlike other student finance, this type of funding doesn't normally have to be paid back

- Funding is available for a wide variety of applicants. For example:
  - Students who are from a disadvantaged background or in severe financial need
  - Students whose academic performance, sporting or musical achievements are excellent; the funding is often to help you keep up these activities
  - If you're studying a specific course or subject
  - Based on where you live or where you're from. If you've moved away to go to uni, this doubles your opportunities: you can apply based on your university town and your home town
  - Based on what your family does for a living or who you're descended from
  - If you need to travel for your course or study or work abroad
  - If you have a disability or if you have dependents who rely on you
  - Funding is also available for a whole host of other reasons and some are quite unusual e.g. if you're a vegetarian or if you're entrepreneurial

You might think that spending a few hours searching for funding and then writing a letter or filling in an application form is a faff. However, if you get paid around £6/hour doing a Saturday job, you'll earn about £40-50 in a day; it would therefore take you around three months to earn the same as a £600 award

Part-Time Paid Work

Consider working part-time. You won't be alone: research shows that around three quarters of students work part-time to help fund their studies.

During term-time you could consider:

- University jobs: look for jobs within departments, the library, the Student Union or as a student ambassador (helping prospective students and their families at open days or help new students at moving-in days)

- Jobs in pubs, cafes or restaurants often come with the added bonus that you get fed too

- Jobs in department stores often give decent staff discounts and you can use it across all the different departments e.g. clothes, shoes, sportswear

- Do you have a skill you can sell? E.g. artwork, academic or music tutoring

If you want to do paid work during the holidays:

- Let previous employers know when you're home and that you'll be happy to work for them

- Look for Christmas jobs well in advance

Try not to rely on a part-time job as your main source of income to fund your living costs. It's unlikely that you'll earn enough money to support yourself and working long shifts will impact your studies. Plus it would leave you with little time to socialise or relax, which is an important part of university life and crucial for your mental health.

If you're an international student, find out whether you're allowed to undertake paid work and, if so, how many hours you're allowed to do.

Fee Waivers

A university might offer a fee waiver - where the university pays part or all of a student's tuition fee.

- Check your university website for criteria e.g. it might be available to those on a low income or students showing exceptional talent

Hardship Funds

You could get emergency cash from your university if you're experiencing financial hardship and are at risk of dropping out.

- You should contact your university student services department to find out if you're eligible

- You'll need to provide evidence and they're unlikely to help if it's simply a case of over-spending

- It's often a once-only payment

Bank Overdraft

You might have opted for a student bank account, which normally has fee-free and interest-free overdraft facilities.

- Try only to go into the overdraft facility of your bank account as an emergency

- Try to avoid going over your overdraft limit as you'll incur additional charges and fees

- Remember, an overdraft is a loan: whatever you borrow has to be paid back. And its rate will increase once you graduate

Emergency Money

Keep £20 in a safe place that you carry on you e.g. in your phone case. Do not touch it. It's there for emergencies e.g. if you lose your purse/wallet or you run out of money or you need to get a taxi home. If you must use it, replace it.

Shop Savvy

You may now be buying some, if not all, of your food, personal and household requirements. Given that you're likely to be on a restricted income, there are some things you should bear in mind.

Before You Go Shopping

- Check your cupboards in advance and write a shopping list - this avoids possible throwing away or having to store duplicate purchases

- Take your own re-usable shopping bags otherwise you're likely to be charged 5p or 10p per bag

- Eat before you go food shopping - it really cuts down on impulse buying

- Keep your receipts in case you need to return or exchange something

- Where possible, use cash rather than a debit or credit card - you're more likely to keep track of your spending

Where to Shop

- It's usually cheaper to buy from a supermarket rather than from a corner or campus shop
  - And look on price comparison sites: some supermarkets routinely feature as being cheaper than others

What to Buy

- Branded items are usually more expensive
  - You should ask yourself if you can tell the difference between the branded and the own-brand version
  - If you can, or if it's important, then go ahead but cut back on your spending somewhere else

- When looking at the cost of items, check the shelf label for the cost per volume e.g. 100g/kg/sheets/tablets etc – not the pack price - and compare that with the alternatives on the shelf. Huge savings can be made. For example:
  - A home brand kitchen roll can be on special offer at £1 per 100 sheets versus a whopping £2.60 per 100 sheets for an alternative version
  - Or a generic version of antihistamine tablets can be £3 for 30 (10p/tablet) while the alternative (branded) version is £3.10 for seven (44.3p/tablet) - yet they contain the same active ingredient

- Frozen vegetables might be a good idea since you won't have to eat them straightaway and they'll last longer than fresh vegetables

- Meat and fish can be the most expensive food ingredients on a shopping list whereas pulses - such as beans, lentils and peas - are some of the cheapest
  - Pulses are low in calories and fat but packed with fibre, vitamins and minerals
  - Use them in dishes to replace some or all of the meat e.g. kidney beans in chilli con carne or chickpeas in a chicken curry
  - Try a few vegetarian meals during the week to keep costs down. Thousands of people regularly take part in meat-free Monday

- It's often cheaper to buy items loose rather than already bagged e.g. fruit and vegetables. And you get to check them for bruises etc

- Look for BOGOF: buy one get one free - maybe you can store or freeze the spare

Deal or Not Such a Good Deal

- Look out for deals/special offers - but always check the price per volume

- It helps to have an idea of what things normally cost so you know if something's really a good deal

- Discount stores might be selling something for £1 but it might be a smaller size and therefore more expensive by volume than the regular size item from elsewhere

When to Buy

- It's often cheaper to buy fresh items at the end of the day when they've been marked down (often identified by their yellow label)

- However, choice will be limited, check for any damage and be sure you'll eat it (or freeze it) before it goes off

Discount Deals

There are a variety of discount deals you could use, for example:

- You could save money on travel by investing in a discount card e.g. 16-25 Railcard, Young Persons Coachcard
  - And you can normally save money on travel tickets by booking train and coach fares in advance

- Discount providers allow you to access a host of savings and many are aimed specifically at students. They might even give you discounts on the purchase of a rail or coach card

- For example, NUS, Save the Student, Unidays and Student Beans

- Sign up for the discount cards where you normally shop e.g. supermarkets or chemists. They often give you money-off vouchers or discounts

- If eating out, look online for 2-for-1 deals

- Offer to be a model/have your hair cut by a trainee at a salon. An experienced hairdresser oversees but you pay a discounted price

- If your phone is unlocked, there are some great SIM-only deals available

Save Money: Alternatives to the Typical Degree

There are a number of different ways you can obtain a university degree and the following will cost you less than if you were to follow the traditional three-year, full-time route.

Accelerated Degree

In January 2019, legislation was passed in the House of Commons to support the expansion of two-year and other accelerated degrees.

- If you opt to study a shorter university course, such as a three-year course condensed into two years, you could:
    - Save 20 per cent on tuition fees compared to a traditional course (studying at a public university)
    - Have one year less maintenance costs
    - Start your career sooner

- Accelerated degrees provide the same level of academic content as traditional degree programmes

- In order to condense the teaching into a shorter time period, the number of teaching hours is likely to be greater so you're likely to have less holiday than students taking the traditional route

- Accelerated degrees have been available in the private sector for some time but this is a new approach in the wider higher education sector. Check online to see which universities and what courses are being offered under the accelerated option

Degree Apprenticeship

Degree apprenticeships are a new type of programme being developed by employers, universities and professional bodies working in partnership.

- If you opt for a degree apprenticeship you'd be employed by an organisation whilst studying for a degree on a part-time basis

- You might attend university on a day-to-day schedule or in blocks of time, depending on the programme and the requirements of your employer

- The benefits of undertaking a degree apprenticeship include:
  - No tuition fee
  - No maintenance loan
  - You'd gain a degree
  - You'd also gain work experience
  - You'd be employed, trained and paid
  - And there's the likelihood of a permanent position on completion

- Degree apprenticeships can take between three to six years to complete, depending on the course level

- For more information and an up-to-date list of current degree vacancy listings:
  - https://www.gov.uk/government/publications/higher-and-degree-apprenticeships

Sponsored Degree

- Students who are sponsored by an organisation may receive a salary or a bursary throughout their degree

- The sponsor may pay some or all of their tuition fees

- Students normally attend university on a full-time basis but undertake paid work for their sponsor during university holidays

- They're likely to be offered - or may be expected to take up - a role within the organisation on graduation

These schemes are pretty competitive so keep an eye on application deadlines. They're more common in certain sectors e.g. finance and business, technology, engineering and the military.

Money Difficulties - Do Not Panic

If you find yourself getting into difficulties with money, speak to:

- Your university student finance/student services department - you may be able to get additional income through grants or the hardship fund

- The bank

- Your parents, grandparents or other family members

- Read through the 'Scholarships, Bursaries, Grants & Awards' section

Don't take out loans without getting advice from your university student finance department. Some loan companies charge phenomenal amounts of interest and you may end up with a bad credit rating - or worse - if you're unable to pay back the required amounts on time.

Repaying Government Loans

For many students, taking out the tuition fee loan and/or the maintenance loan for every year of your studies is a sobering thought. On paper, this looks like a significant amount of money: tuition fee and maintenance loans combined can amount to borrowings in the region of £50,000+.

However, it's important to remember that, the way repayments currently work, many students will re-pay only a small amount of what they owe and some will re-pay nothing at all.

For most UK undergraduate students, studying in England and Wales, the following currently applies:

- Repayments don't start until April, the year after you graduate from university

- You only start repayments once you're earning above a certain salary threshold: currently £25,725 (April 2019)
    - So if you earn less than this, you won't repay anything towards your loans

- The amount you pay back is 9% of the income you earn over the salary threshold. For example:
    - If you earn £27,725 a year then you are £2,000 over the current threshold
    - 9% of £2,000 is £180 a year so you will pay £15 each month towards your student loans
    - If you dip below £25,725 then repayments will stop

- Repayments are automatically made through the tax system

- Repayments will stop if you have paid off your loan, are normally written off after 30 years, or if you become permanently disabled or die

- For more information, read the guidance on repaying loans provided by your loan provider

These are useful resources for everything concerning student finance:

- https://www.gov.uk/browse/education/student-finance

- Save the Student: https://www.savethestudent.org

8

Staying Safe at University

Keeping You & Your Belongings Safe

There are lots of things you can do to keep yourself and your belongings safe whilst you're at university. For example:

- Use locks and keys:
    - Use lock codes on all your devices e.g. on your phone and computer
    - Close entry doors behind you when you enter residential buildings
    - Don't allow people into residential buildings unless you know them
    - Lock your home's doors and windows securely when you leave
    - If you have a bike, lock it securely when not in use - even if it's inside your home

- Insure your belongings

- Back up your devices in case they're lost or stolen

- Stay safe on nights out:

- Make sure your phone is fully charged before you go out
- Have the telephone number of a reputable taxi firm in your phone (your university may have a list of recommended firms)
- Try not to withdraw cash from machines at night
- Make plans in advance to go home with someone you trust
- Look out for each other: agree with your friends that no-one is left alone or behind
- Travel with friends rather than on your own and don't let friends go home alone, especially if they're drunk
- If travelling on public transport, sit near the driver or sit in a busy carriage. If you feel uncomfortable, move
- Don't take short cuts through quiet or dodgy areas - it's better to take the brighter, well-lit, busier route even if takes you a bit longer
- Keep a look out for anyone who looks like they're in an uncomfortable situation or losing control and tell the bar staff or whoever appears to be in charge

Alcohol

Alcohol tends to be a big part of university life - especially when you first arrive - and there may be a drinking culture at the university or within some clubs and societies.

- You might experience pressure to drink - from people around you or from yourself - so that you feel you fit in. It's important to remember that it's okay not to drink to excess or not to drink at all

- If you're a non-drinker, you're not alone: a survey by the National Union of Students in 2018 found that 21% of students don't drink alcohol

- And, in order to meet the increased demand amongst low or non-drinking students, the number of alcohol-free events (sometimes known as Sober Socials) run by universities, student unions and clubs and societies are increasing, as are alcohol-free student halls

Impact of Alcohol

A person who has a normal tolerance for alcohol might find, after drinking 1 or 2 units, they experience feeling warm, sociable and talkative.

However, more than that can have a variety of negative effects, such as:

- Your judgment and reasoning are affected, meaning you're more likely to lose self-control, become reckless, uninhibited or put yourself in a risky situation

- It can make you feel light headed, it can impair your memory, and reaction times and co-ordination can be affected

- It can affect your balance, make you slur or vomit - none of which is a good look

- Alcohol irritates your digestive system and can cause stomach pain, vomiting and diarrhoea

- It can make you vulnerable and there are people who'll take advantage of this e.g. they might steal your stuff, hurt you or be intimate with you without your consent

- If you're feeling low or stressed, you may be tempted to drink more alcohol - but alcohol is a depressant so any feelings can be worsened. And an underlying mental disorder may also be worsened by alcohol use

- Your sleep is impacted: you'll get fewer hours of deep sleep, alcohol's a diuretic so your sleep will be disturbed as you'll need to go to the loo in the night, and you'll lose fluid through sweat so you'll be dehydrated. All in all, you'll wake feeling tired and groggy the next day

- Too much too often can lead to a red, puffy face and a bloated stomach

You're Not Drinking?

There are a number of good reasons for not drinking alcohol. If you feel that you need to explain why you're not drinking, you could say:

- You don't like the taste of it

- You don't like how it makes you feel

- For cultural reasons

- For health reasons e.g. a medication you're on is affected by alcohol

- You're sporty or health conscious. Alcohol is made from sugar or starch so it's full of 'empty' calories i.e. they have no nutritional value

- You have a sports event, deadline or early morning lecture so you need a clear head the next day

- It's too expensive

Whatever reason you have it's perfectly fine not to drink much or any alcohol. Over time, you should find that people will accept you as you are. You'll probably drift towards alcohol-free events and befriend other non-drinkers.

Initiations

Some clubs and societies encourage excessive drinking - usually followed by humiliating rituals - amongst new members at initiations.

Some people think it's a laugh but some people are scared of initiations - of the volume of alcohol they know they'll be expected to consume and the actions they'll be expected to perform. There's no doubt about how dangerous excessive drinking can be.

There have been a number of deaths associated with initiations including that of Ed Farmer, a Newcastle University student who died after an Agricultural Society initiation in 2016. Ed was found at 4am, collapsed in the corridor of a student house, five times over the legal alcohol limit, his clothes soaked through and his head shaved. Although his friends took him to hospital, he suffered a cardiac arrest and was pronounced brain dead.

There have been other deaths in the UK after such ceremonies, including Gavin Britton at Exeter University, Tom Ward at Hull University and Alex Doji at Staffordshire University.

Universities are aware that these ceremonies take place, know how dangerous they are and most, if not all, forbid those involving excessive drinking. However some clubs and societies (arguing that it's 'tradition' or a 'harmless rite of passage') respond by carrying them out under the radar. For example, by conducting them off campus, telling students not to tell anyone outside the club or society, or telling them not to bring any ID (as happened to Ed Farmer).

Students, clubs and societies that choose to be involved in banned initiations can face serious consequences:

- In 2018, Northumbria University issued formal warnings and withdrew a number of elite sports scholarships from those involved in the football team's initiation involving alcohol

- Also in 2018, UCL Students' Union shut down its men's rugby club, withdrew its funding, prevented the team from training on the university pitches and removed the team from the university league after team members attempted to hold a banned initiation ceremony. In an attempt to prevent the Union finding out, the club had told attendees to sign non-disclosure agreements but it was, nevertheless, reported to the Union

You have choices:

- You don't have to participate in these types of ceremonies

- You don't have to drink everything or do everything

- If you decide to go then read the advice above: Strategies for Managing a Night Out

- If you feel that you'd only be accepted if you joined in, but you really don't want to, then consider looking for an alternative club. They're not all the same
    - Look for a similar club or society on campus that doesn't have the same reputation or 'rules'. They might have initiations but ones which are fun rather than cruel, excessive or undignified
    - You could look for the same club or society in the nearest town

Strategies for Managing a Night Out

If you know you're going to be drinking heavily, there are things you can do to manage its impact better. These include:

- Eating a proper meal and having a large glass of water before you start drinking

- Not going crazy at the 'pre' otherwise you'll peak early then be a mess half way through the night

- Drinking slowly

- Drinking water or soft drinks throughout the evening as well as alcohol

- Not drinking everything or at every round: refuse it, go to the loo, stay on the dance floor, mix it, replace it with water, spill it or pour it away

- Eating whilst drinking

- Managing yourself: you know how much alcohol you can tolerate so limit yourself to a number of drinks per hour

- Not drinking to the point that you can't make sensible decisions e.g. lose your phone, fall over, vomit, get in a fight, snog someone you'll regret the following day, end up in A&E

- Leaving out a large bottle of water by your bed - and drinking it before you go to sleep

Drugs

It's possible that you'll come across drugs at university and you may be invited to take them.

The Risks

Risks associated with taking drugs without medical supervision include:

- It's illegal therefore the drugs are unregulated: you can never be sure what they contain or what the effects might be
  - To make them go further, they could be mixed with other drugs or toxic substances
  - Or they may be in a purer form and therefore far stronger than something similar that you - or someone you know - may have taken previously

- You can't be sure how you might react to them - everyone is different

- There are known links between drug use and mental health problems: either developing a serious mental health disorder or worsening an underlying one

- They can be highly addictive and, over time, a person might have to take the drug just to feel 'normal' and they might have a hard time controlling their need to take the drug
    - Some people might start to feel the need to take more of a drug or take it more often, and it can impact their sleeping and eating patterns and social interactions. They might borrow or steal money to pay for the drugs

- Universities are increasingly carrying out random drug raids in university accommodation - using sniffer dogs, cocaine swabs and body-cams
    - Students found with drugs may be expelled, evicted or arrested

How to Say No

The organisation FRANK provides honest information on drugs. If you're feeling pressured to take drugs - and you don't want to - suggestions from FRANK include:

- Prepare yourself. Think about how you'd like to respond if someone offers you drugs so you know what to say

- Say no firmly but clearly and without making a big deal about it. If someone tries to persuade you, don't feel like you have to change your mind

- You're not alone. It's easy to think you're the only one who's not tried drugs but, actually, most young people don't take drugs

- If you're finding it hard to be yourself within your group, take a step back and think about whether it's time to find a new group of people to hang out with

Source: www.talktofrank.com
FRANK's confidential helpline, open 24/7, is 0300 123 6600

Smoking/Vaping

Traditional Cigarettes

You know there's nothing good about smoking. Your breath smells, it stains your teeth, it ages your skin, weakens your bones, you smell, it's expensive, it's the largest cause of cancer and it increases your likelihood of a heart attack or stroke.

- Give up smoking. Some people find it difficult to give up, especially as nicotine is addictive. But there's support available to help you: you can access the NHS Stopping Smoking Service through places such as community pharmacies and NHS GP surgeries

- Put any money you would have spent on cigarettes into a glass pot like a jam jar, and watch it quickly grow. Then reward yourself with something lovely because you deserve it: it's not easy to kick an addiction

E-cigarettes

E-cigarettes allow you to inhale nicotine in a vapour. Although less harmful than smoking conventional cigarettes, they aren't harmless.

- They contain nicotine, which is known to be an addictive substance and one that raises your heart rate

- The vapour contains some potentially harmful chemicals

- There are many unknowns about vaping including the long-term impact on health

Don't take up e-cigarettes if you're a non-smoker. But if you're trying to stop smoking conventional cigarettes, current Government recommendations are that e-cigarettes are a useful aid, particularly in conjunction with expert help such as the NHS Stopping Smoking Service.

"Remember not everyone is having a great time all the time and it's alright to have some down days, everyone has them"

(Female, age 18)

9

Feeling Stressed, Worried, Overwhelmed, Lonely or Worse

New Student Blues

Starting university can be an exciting time but even the most confident person can feel some anxiety given the many new situations they'll experience and the many new people they'll meet.

It's quite common to feel low at different points in time, for example, when you're missing the good old days - old friends, old routines, having things done for you - or dealing with new challenges such as managing your money, new ways of working, or dealing with flatmate or friendship issues.

Going to university *is* an unusual situation. For eighteen years, most of you will have lived at home with family and friends around you - people who know you inside out. Starting university, however, thrusts you into new surroundings. The workload may be intense, you may have too little (or too much) free time, you're mixing with and trying to find friends amongst people you don't know, you might be having to look after yourself, you might be worrying about money, and you might feel pressure to have a great time.

When I asked, in my research, what first year students liked least about being at university, there were four common themes:

- Study stresses

- Money worries

- Feeling overwhelmed

- Their emotional wellbeing - particularly feeling lonely, sad and homesick

Study Stresses

People often talk about the social element of going to university - going out, making friends, drinking, late nights, clubbing, etc - but most university courses actually require a considerable amount of work. And the responsibility is now on your shoulders to stay organised and focused as the teaching staff aren't likely to chase you or monitor the progression of your assignments.

- Studying at university - even when you've taken the subject at A level - is usually a step up in terms of content, complexity and volume. First year students in my research said this was one aspect they disliked about being at university:

"Managing the workload"
(Female, age 19)

"Revision for tests and weekly assignments"
(Male, age 19)

"The workload and short deadlines"
(Male, age 19)

"The workload is really intense"
(Female, age 18)

- The teaching approaches at university can be different to what you're used to

"The change in teaching methods where you are guided far less so I find it difficult to know which bits of the course to focus on"
(Male, age 19)

"Independent work and less guidance"
(Female, age 19)

- Contact time with teaching staff - lectures, seminars, tutorials, labs and practicals - varies widely, usually by course. Having too little free time, or conversely having too much, requires discipline on your behalf

- Class sizes might be large, which might make asking questions difficult

There are lots of strategies to help you manage your studies better.

- Do start preparing assignments early so you have time to ask any questions or deal with anything that might delay handing in a paper

"Do work early so you don't have to be up ridiculous hours to get it done"
(Female, age 18)

- Don't let assignments stack up - this only adds to the stress. As the students in my research said: another paper or test is likely to be following closely behind

- Do ask teaching staff and other students for help if you're not sure about something - you're invariably not the only one who didn't understand

- Do attend all your lectures - and definitely follow-up what you miss
  - You may find that your tutors record lectures, enabling you to catch up any you've missed or review content you found confusing

- Read the background material or do the preparation that's been suggested by teaching staff - the lecture is just one part of the information you need

- If teaching staff suggests an assignment will take four weeks, that's how much time you're supposed to allocate to it

- Keep track of all your deadlines in a planner or diary

- Manage your time carefully if your course is intense
  - Subjects such as engineering, law or medicine often require you to spend a lot of hours in class and you'll be left with limited time to do everything else
  - You'll need to be extra organised and focused so there's time to enjoy your life outside your course

- Manage yourself if your course is lesson-light
  - Students on courses with relatively little contact time, for example, politics, business studies or English literature, are expected to undertake a lot of independent study
  - This is a huge change from school or college - where you may have had only a few 'frees' each week - and it might take a little while to get used to being self-directed so that you don't waste time or fall behind on reading or preparatory work
  - In your diary, timetable your reading, research and preparation time rather than have lots of blank spaces that look like free time
  - If you feel you can easily manage all your work in the allocated time then perhaps do other things, for example, get a part-time job (good for money and for your CV), learn a language, take up a sport or volunteer to help run a club or society

- Take advantage of any resources the university offers: from the library to skills workshops to buddy systems

- Don't plagiarise: universities are known to use sophisticated computer programmes to scan work for evidence of plagiarism

- Don't spend all your time studying: make time for relaxation and the social aspects of being at university. This is an important part of the university experience and crucial for your mental wellbeing

- Speak to your personal tutor if you feel worried about your course - they're there to support you

- Apply all the study tips that got you to university in the first place

Money Worries

It's not uncommon for students to have money worries.

- This might be the first time that you've had to live on a restricted income and you might find it hard to budget

- Most of you will try to live within your means and attempt to control how much money you borrow

- If you're living away from home, there's likely to be a realisation about how much things cost and how much your parents previously paid for

- And the maintenance loan may not be sufficient - even to pay your rent

In my research, the first year students commonly mentioned the lack of money as one of the main things they liked least about being at university: having to live on a restricted income, having loans, building up debts, and worrying about money in general.

Comments included:

"Being poor"
(Female, age 18)

"Debt"
(Female, age 20)

"Budgeting"
(Male, age 18)

"Money not enough of it"
(Female, age 18)

"Having to worry about how much you're spending"
(Female, age 18)

"Realising how much everything costs/having to pay for everything you didn't consider before"
(Male, age 19)

For some of you, the maintenance loan combined with any other income you have, e.g. parental contribution or savings, may not be sufficient to live on.

- If you have money worries, read Chapter 7: Money - especially the section on scholarships, grants, bursaries and awards, fee waivers and hardship funds.

- There are pots of money available, particularly if you're experiencing financial hardship. You just need to know where to look

- Also, read the section on paying off Government loans. It's important to remember that, the way repayments currently work, many students will re-pay only a small amount of what they owe and some will re-pay nothing at all

Feeling Overwhelmed

Since the majority of you will move away from home to attend university, some or all of the domestic tasks must now be done by you.

On top of attending lectures and undertaking coursework, you might be shopping, cooking, cleaning, doing laundry, socialising, taking part in sport, training and society events, keeping up with old friends and possibly a partner from home. And maybe doing paid work too. So it's not unreasonable that you might feel besieged by tasks, overcome with tiredness and feel you have no time to relax.

This sense of being overwhelmed was frequently commented on, in my research, as one of the things that first year students liked least about being at university:

"Stress! Keeping on top of all aspects of your life (food, money, cleaning, socialising and of course work)"
(Male, age 20)

"The lack of time for yourself and to relax"
(Female, age 18)

"Having to prepare meals when I'm tired"
(Female, age 18)

"Having to do your own washing"
(Female, age 18)

"Cooking and cleaning"
(Male, age 18)

"Having to do everything for myself"
(Female, age 18)

There are various things you can do to help manage your busy schedule better.

- If you're living away from home
    - Learn from your flatmates: what do they cook that's tasty, quick, healthy and easy? What shortcuts do they use?
    - Could you take turns with a flatmate or friend? E.g. preparing and cooking a meal, doing a load of laundry, having a cleaning rota
    - Try online shopping instead of going to the shops. It's much quicker. Although you might need to do it ahead of time as delivery slots might not be available for a few days

- If you know you have a deadline or a test the following day then it's okay to miss one night out - there will be plenty more

- If it seems the coursework is taking you longer than it should, speak to your tutor or investigate workshops or buddy systems. They might be able to suggest tips you could try

- If you're drinking, manage your alcohol intake
    - Don't drink every night and don't drink if you have a deadline or a test the following day - you won't sleep well and it'll affect your performance
    - It's also expensive. Instead, perhaps you could have friends over to watch a film, game or play cards

- If you're doing paid work, could you reduce your hours?
    - If you need the money, read Chapter 7: Money - particularly bursaries, grants, scholarships and awards, fee waivers and hardship funds

- Take occasional rests and time away from everyone and everything
    - It's okay to say no. When your life is very busy, time alone (ideally with the phone off) is good for the soul and can help you re-charge

- You could listen to music, read for pleasure, watch a bit of TV, maybe do some yoga, go for a run in the fresh air, game or simply potter

- This sense of feeling overwhelmed is particularly common amongst Freshers in their first term when you're acclimatising to university life plus everyone is eager to go out and socialise
  - You should find that you get a bit more efficient at domestic tasks
  - Hopefully you'll become quicker at doing coursework as you use all the resources that are available
  - And the pressure to join in and go to everything should get a bit less as time passes

Loneliness, Sadness and Homesickness

Feeling lonely, sad and homesick are common feelings amongst new students. Know that you're not alone and, for most students, over time you'll become more settled and those feelings will pass.

Amongst the first year students in my research, when I asked about what they liked least about being at university, there were many responses that focused on their emotional wellbeing, including:

"It's quite easy to feel lonely"
(Female, age 18)

"Loneliness"
(Male, age 19)

"Being away from close friends and family"
(Female, age 19)

"Missing home comforts"
(Female, age 19)

There are things that you can do, which could help:

- Talk about how you're feeling: you may find others around you are experiencing the same emotions or they might share how they're dealing with these feelings. Remember: you're all new together

- Go along to a few clubs or societies that you might be interested in. Not only will this provide a distraction but you're likely to make new contacts and friends

- Look on your university website: there may be initiatives specifically aimed at welcoming and integrating new students

- Look after your physical health
    - Eat and drink healthily: this affects us emotionally as well as physically (read Chapter 5: Food & Drink)
    - Get sufficient sleep: not getting enough sleep can affect your ability to concentrate, your ability to memorise things and you're more likely to be irritable and behave impulsively. Try to prepare your mind and body for sleep e.g. have a warm bath or shower, read a book or listen to the radio, turn off screens, write a 'to do' list, do some light stretches, make the room dark and quiet (invest in ear plugs, if necessary)
    - Exercise: isn't just good for the body, it can also be a social activity, it helps you sleep, and the endorphins released during exercise can reduce pain and boost happiness. Try to do at least 30 minutes of moderate aerobic activity five days a week - perhaps incorporate it into your daily routine such as walking briskly or cycling to class - and do strength exercises on two or more days a week
    - Cut down or stop any alcohol, drugs and smoking: read Chapter 8 on why these things are not good for you and why you should cut them down/out - not only for your health but it would help with any financial worries

- Family and old friends
  - Do speak to your family and old friends - they can be a wonderful, reassuring, supportive network. They're likely to be missing you and will be delighted to speak to you
  - Try not to go home too early. Give yourself time to get used to things. Some universities recommend not going home for the first month
  - But, booking a trip home - just knowing that it's planned - can take a bit of pressure off you and lift your spirits
  - Instead of going home, you could invite friends and family to visit so you can show them your new surroundings. You might experience a sense of pride showing them your room, the university, the facilities and the local area

- Social media: recognise that it's life through a filter
  - Looking at other people's social media can make you feel low, make you feel bad about yourself and create FOMO (a fear of missing out)
  - When friends' posts show them having the most amazing time at university, you might feel it's only you who's not having #thebesttimeever. As commented on by students in my research:

"It's so easy to become someone who thinks that others are having a far better time. Social media is the main cause of this."
(Female, age 19)

"The social expectations and pressure to make friends instantly and comparing your experiences to others through social media"
(Female, age 18)

  - Remember that people tend to carefully curate their posts e.g. when they're looking their best or they're in a fun place. They don't tend to include the majority of their time: the everyday, the mundane, the boring

- Even your own posts might suggest you're having the most brilliant time - even if you're not

- But social media can also be a force for good. For example:
  - It enables you to communicate with other people remotely and helps maintain existing relationships when you're geographically distant from each other - therefore helping you to feel less lonely and isolated
  - People commonly discuss, in real life, what they've seen online - so it's something to talk about
  - And, because of the anonymity it can offer, you can communicate with other people who have the same interests as you without a fear of being stigmatised

- Let the university know if you need support
  - The university lecturers, personal tutors and support staff have seen many of these same struggles before and can help you: they'll listen, make useful suggestions and support you
  - They may be able to offer practical help to immediately relieve any stress you're experiencing e.g. offer to extend a coursework deadline, allow you extra time in exams, or offer one-to-one support from a tutor
  - Some universities offer mentoring schemes or support groups
  - There may be student-led support services. Although the students may not be qualified counsellors, you may prefer to talk about problems such as stress and depression with another student
  - Your university might run a Nightline service: an anonymous listening and information service run by students for students from 7pm-8am during term-time
  - Most universities have welfare teams who can provide independent and confidential advice and guidance to students on academic, welfare and personal issues
  - You could approach the staff at the chaplaincy/multi-faith centre on site

Some good advice from the students in my research:

"Remember not everyone is having a great time all the time and it's alright to have some down days, everyone has them"
(Female, age 18)

"Have realistic expectations, everyone has different experiences and don't worry if your experience doesn't match up to someone else's"
(Male, age 19)

"Don't go into uni life with any preconceptions - the likelihood is that you won't make friends straight away, you will feel lonely and you will miss school friends."
(Male, age 18)

"Keep your home friends close – keep FaceTiming them throughout as it helps if you're feeling slightly lonely or need advice only they can give you"
(Female, age 19)

"It gets better, just stick it out. Say yes"
(Female, age 18)

"When things get tough, they do get better. It's better to stick things out at uni than go home every weekend"
(Female, age 18)

Be kind to yourself. Going to university is a whole new way of being and you're just getting used it. The first term is likely to be the hardest as you adjust, find your feet and your friends. Don't give up, give it time.

During the Christmas break you'll probably find that you're missing new friends and you're very likely to miss the independence and freedom that you've become used to.

If Things Become More Serious: Getting Professional Help

Whether you have pre-existing mental health needs or you feel that things have escalated to a point where they're affecting your daily life, it's important to know that help is available.

- Seek help early if you do experience a problem with your mental health at university - you don't need to wait or try to handle things on your own

- And know that you're not alone. In 2018, the BBC reviewed data from 83 UK universities and found that over 78,000 students sought help from university mental health services in 2017

Some possible signs of escalating emotional difficulty could include persistent sadness, anxiety or depression; feelings of apathy towards things you used to enjoy; weight changes; excessive studying or missing lectures and deadlines; increased isolation; poor personal hygiene; hair loss; insomnia or sleeping too much; and self-harm.

There are things you can do, which could help:

- Look on your university website. Most universities have a free and confidential in-house counselling service where you can access professionally qualified counsellors, psychotherapists and mental health advisers

- Speak to your GP

- There are external organisations where you can find support and advice, for example:
    - Mind: 0300 123 3393 (lines are open 9am to 6pm, Monday to Friday except for bank holidays) or email info@mind.org.uk or text 86463

- Student Minds: https://www.studentminds.org.uk/findsupport.html or email info@studentminds.org.uk
- The Samaritans: 116 123 (you can call for FREE any time from any phone, even a mobile without credit, this number won't show up on your phone bill) or email jo@samaritans.org or visit www.samaritans.org to find details of your nearest branch, where you can talk to a trained volunteer face-to-face
- PAPYRUS HOPELINEUK: 0800 068 41 41, text 07786 209 697 or email pat@papyrus-uk.org

If you're in crisis now, call 999 or go to your nearest hospital A&E (Accident and Emergency) department

Worried About a Friend

Perhaps a friend has told you they're unhappy or you've noticed some changes in their appearance or behaviour (see possible signs of emotional struggle opposite).

- If you're worried about a friend's emotional wellbeing, you could let them know you're concerned about them, ask them how they're feeling and include them in social arrangements - they'll appreciate this

- If they're seriously struggling, however, it's important to know your own limits
    - Although you can offer help, you're unlikely to have the expertise, the experience or the resources that a professionally trained person has
    - Also, you shouldn't be your friend's sole source of support and you do need to be clear about how much you can help

- Encourage your friend to speak to their family or other friends, access professional help through the university support team and/or their GP and/or use the external resources above

- If you're very concerned for your friend, you could approach a tutor who can make the university support team aware that a student needs help

- Also, it can be stressful supporting someone who has mental health needs so you should make sure that you keep up your own interests and relationships and ensure you're properly supported too
  - You could talk to a friend (who doesn't gossip), a member of your family, access support from the university or use the external resources above

Resources you might find useful:

www.nhs.uk/conditions/stress-anxiety-depression/student-mental-health/
www.nhs.uk/conditions/stress-anxiety-depression/student-stress/
www.mind.org.uk/information-support/tips-for-everyday-living/student-life/#.XMBL5jBKjIU
https://www.studentminds.org.uk/findsupport.html
www.samaritans.org
https://papyrus-uk.org
www.studentsagainstdepression.org

If You're Considering Leaving

If you're very unhappy, feel that you aren't settling at university and are considering leaving, there are things you can do.

- It might help to set a time to review the situation e.g. at the end of term
  - Setting a time may take some pressure off you
  - You might also find that, by then, you're settled; it does take time for everyone to get used to being at university

- If you're able, you should discuss this with your parents so they can support you

- Talk to your personal tutor or department staff
  - They'll help you explore your options and advise you on your next steps: whether it's ways they can help you right now or whether it's transferring to another course within the same university, changing university or leaving higher education altogether

- If being away from home is the issue then you could consider transferring to a university closer to home

- Perhaps university is right for you but the timing is wrong
  - You may be able to defer for a year, i.e. halt your studies at a point in the year, then return to the same point one year later

- If money is a concern then you could read Chapter 7: Money. You'll find suggestions of how to apply for additional funding but also alternatives to the typical degree. You could also consider studying on a part-time basis

- If you'd like to transfer to a different course or study at a different university it might affect your student loan (if you have one) so you should contact your loan provider

- Check the terms of any Government grant you may have received since you may have to make repayments if you leave the course early (check with the provider)

- And know that university doesn't suit everyone
  - If you decide it's not for you, there are other ways to forge ahead with your career, become successful and be fulfilled
  - Take that same focus and determination that got you into university in the first place and apply it to whatever you decide to do next. Good luck!

If your son or daughter moves away from home to go to university, you will - over time - get used to the new normal

10

The Parents' Chapter

Emotional Impact

If your son or daughter moves away from home to attend university, it can be difficult for you, emotionally.

You may have witnessed them becoming more independent as they reached 18. They may have started (legally) going to bars and nightclubs; they may have passed their driving test and started driving themselves and their friends to places (scary); they may have started earning their own money and making their own purchases (great - although some you might disapprove of); and they may have headed off to festivals and holidays with their friends (more worry).

But parents are on the periphery of these full and busy lives and you may have been used to - and enjoyed - the noise and excitement that comes with older teenagers.

Also, the focus has been sharply on them throughout A levels and then Results Day.

If the offer of a university place was conditional on achieving certain grades then, after getting their results, there's a flurry of activity, which includes:

- Confirming their university
    - If they got the results they needed then accepting an offer from their first (firm) or back-up (insurance) choice university
    - If they didn't get the results they needed, they may have chosen an alternative course or university through UCAS Clearing
    - If their results were better than expected, they may have opted for a different course or university altogether through the UCAS Adjustment service

- Followed by the emails from the university

- The emails concerning finances

- If they're leaving home, there's the excitement (and fear) surrounding where they'll be living and who their new flatmates will be

- Followed by all the preparing and shopping, which you (and your credit card) are likely to be heavily involved in. Hundreds of pounds and many hours are likely to be spent on getting all their stuff together (see the lists of suggested items throughout this guide)

- And then they're saying goodbye to friends and family
    - If their friends are going to a variety of universities, the start dates will vary therefore farewell parties will extend over several weeks
    - And, if they're moving away from a partner, then they're likely to want to spend a lot of time with him or her before they leave

With Results Day being just a month or so before they leave, a lot happens in a very short space of time.

And then they're gone.

Staying Connected

If your son or daughter leaves home, how much contact you have with them will vary according to their personality and their experience of being at university.

- If they're naturally a bit more cautious, or if they're finding things a bit hard, then they might contact you frequently - particularly in the beginning - looking for reassurance whilst they get used to university life

- Be positive for them. If they feel lonely, sad or homesick, reassure them that they're not the only one feeling this way, their new life will settle down and things will get better. You could suggest they read Chapter 9

- Maybe they want less contact because they're relishing the independence and freedom that comes from living away from home. They're enjoying finding things out for themselves

- Or maybe they're simply too busy to call or text, especially at the beginning
    - In the first few weeks they're spending time getting to know their new flatmates; going to various events, especially during Freshers' Week; probably going to bed late and then getting up late; making some or all of their own meals - which requires planning, shopping, cooking and cleaning up
    - If they've joined clubs and societies then they're attending the events associated with these interests and going to training sessions if they're sporty
    - They're keeping up with old friends
    - And, if they're in an existing relationship, it will require significant time and commitment to keep it going from a distance
    - Oh, and they've started their course and are working on assignments
    - Life is full on. And you might be low on the 'need to contact' list

- It's possible that the occasional contact you receive might be purely functional in nature e.g. they need to know how to do something or ask if you would pay for something and, as soon as you've explained/resolved it, they may need to go

- You should call and text them occasionally so they know that you're thinking of them
  - You can use social media, e.g. set up a family WhatsApp or Twitter, for everyone to communicate through, and ask them to post the occasional text or photo so you know they're alive
  - You could ask to be accepted as a Friend or Follower on social media so you can see their posts (they may refuse)

- You could set a regular date and time to speak

But the ball is really in their court.

As the weeks pass, their lives calm down and become a bit more routine, you might find that you get more regular contact. Which is nice.

Help for Sad Parents

When a child leaves home for university, parents might experience a sense of loss, similar to grief.

You're used to having them around, you're used to their noise and mess and you're used to being asked for, or about, things. Now contact may be irregular, missing completely, or you may be worried about how they're coping.

As long as you get the sense they're settling in, then the focus should now be on you. You could:

- Talk to other parents whose children have also left for university: share your experiences, they're likely to be similar and they might have some useful coping strategies

- Join support groups - either in real life or online - for parents of new students

- Try not to be sad when you speak to your child
    - Be positive and reassuring if they're feeling a bit wobbly
    - Try not to transfer your own sadness or anxiety

- Start enjoying the freedom that one less child brings e.g. focus on your career, spend more time with your partner, see friends more often, start a new project, fill your life with enjoyable things

- After the initial shock, you do get used to them not being around

- And you will still see them
    - They may come back occasionally during term time for family or friends' events or simply to rest and re-charge
    - And the holidays are frequent and long

Help for Worried Parents

For most parents, there's nothing worse than seeing your child distressed or unhappy.

- If they tell you they're feeling sad, lonely, homesick, overwhelmed or worried, these are common emotions amongst new students (read Chapter 9 to see they're not alone - and suggestions for what to do). Things do tend to settle down and they do normally get better

- If you're concerned he or she is struggling and needs extra support, encourage them to speak to their personal tutor or student support services

- They're familiar with these types of worries and can give your son or daughter good advice and strategies for dealing with their concerns

- If they've moved away from home, encourage them to stay at the university rather than come home often - some universities recommend students don't go home during the first month

- If they continue to struggle, you should maintain regular contact and perhaps set a deadline, for example, at the end of term, to review the situation

- If your son or daughter has told you something or is behaving in a way that's particularly worrying then you should contact the university
    - Student mental health is taken seriously and there's usually an email address or a telephone number on the university's website for worried parents
    - The university will normally arrange for someone from the student welfare department to contact your son or daughter
    - Call 999 if you feel it's life-threatening

Financial Implications

If your son or daughter is from the UK, they can apply to the government for a maintenance loan to go towards living costs.

- How much maintenance loan they get depends on various factors e.g. where they're studying, whether they're living at home or not, whether they're studying full- or part-time

- The maintenance loan, if they're eligible, is partly based on the family household income so there's an implicit expectation that families should contribute towards their child's living costs

- As a guide, you could make up the shortfall between the maintenance loan that your son or daughter receives and the maximum maintenance loan

- For example, for a full-time undergraduate student from England:
    - The maximum maintenance loan in 2019/20 for a student living away from home, outside London is £8,944
    - If your child receives £6,944 in maintenance loan then you could, if you are able, contribute £2,000 per year towards their living costs

- If you're able to contribute more this would be helpful since many students find it difficult to live on this level of income

- Having a son or daughter at university might be financially difficult for you. You may not be in a position to contribute towards their living costs but you do need to have this conversation with your son or daughter in advance: how much, if anything, you can give them and how often they will receive it

- Since the maintenance loan they receive may not be sufficient to even pay their rent, you should discuss other ways they could support themselves financially (see Chapter 7: Money). There are pots of money out there and this chapter shows your son or daughter where to look for them

- In general, it's not recommended that you take out a personal loan to help your child with their student debt. This is almost always a more expensive option than your child taking out a student loan - since interest rates on student loans are still relatively low and, crucially, they only need to repay the loan if they earn enough

The table below shows the maintenance loan for full-time students from England for the academic year 2019/20.

Full-time student	2019 to 2020
Living at home	Up to £7,529
Living away from home, outside London	Up to £8,944
Living away from home, in London	Up to £11,672
Student spends a year of a UK course studying abroad	Up to £10,242

Source: https://www.gov.uk/student-finance/new-fulltime-students

Follow this link for a handy student finance calculator for students from England or the EU starting a new undergraduate course. It estimates student loans and extra state funding. The result will be more accurate if you know your annual household income:

- www.gov.uk/student-finance-calculator

Follow these links for information on student loans:

- England: www.gov.uk/student-finance
- Scotland: www.saas.gov.uk
- Wales: www.studentfinancewales.co.uk
- Northern Ireland: www.studentfinanceni.co.uk

Weekend and Holiday Visits: What to Expect

You're looking forward to seeing them, having them home and hearing all about university life…

- They might turn up tired, grumpy or emotional

- A calm home might become chaotic: there might be squabbling with siblings, arguments over use of the car, loud music playing, doors banging, queues for the bathroom and no food in the fridge

- You might see very little of them. If they're exhausted (physically and emotionally) they might simply want to sleep, they might have come home to see old friends or a partner, they might want to just spend time with the dog

- They might behave as if they're still at university: coming and going at all hours or just staying in their room

They might not want to conform to old rules. They've tasted freedom and they've learnt to live independently of you

- You'll probably have to negotiate new ways of living together:
    - Have a conversation about what you'd like them to do, how you'd like them to behave or what things you'd like help with whilst they're at home
    - Consider not setting curfews but ask them to let you know if they're coming home late, having friends to stay or not coming home at all
    - You can set mutually respectful house rules, e.g. being quiet when others are sleeping
    - Remind them that you and their siblings would like to see them too - so to set some afternoons or evenings aside to catch up

You should let them set their own schedules - as they're used to doing at university. If you're too stifling, you run the risk of them returning to university early or not wanting to come home at all

- They're probably missing home comforts
    - They're very likely to enjoy some favourite meals, with any leftover portions sent back to university with them

- If they're trying to save money then they might bring home large bags of laundry

- You might see them noticeably relaxing into their own bed
  - If you can, it's helpful if their bed or bedroom remains theirs so that they have somewhere secure and comforting to come home to during this time of intense change

- Hopefully you get the sense they're settling in to their new life
  - You might notice, over the Christmas break, that they talk a lot about their new friends and their new life and, by January, they might be keen to re-claim their independence
  - After a few days or weeks of having them home, you too might be looking forward to them re-claiming their independence ;-)

- Christmas and Easter holidays are long: usually lasting around four weeks
  - It's possible that your son or daughter might feel a little anxious about going back to university after such a long break: re-connecting with friends who are still quite new to them, returning to exams, anticipating the chores they'll need to do if they live away from home
  - Be positive for them: talk about all the good things they've mentioned about being at university. It's likely that, after just a few days of being back at university, they'll be completely at ease again
  - If they're returning by car, and if you're able, they'll probably appreciate some food supplies to see them through the first few days

NB Half terms tend not to be the norm at university. Some have Reading Weeks mid-way through the term but the university may expect students to stay in order to do preparatory work or catch up on reading.

Useful Things To Do Before They Leave

If your son or daughter is leaving home, you can take practical steps to help them prepare for independent living. For example:

- Teach them some basic cookery skills, especially meals that are healthy, tasty, quick and easy

- Show them how to do laundry - at least how to use the washing machine

- Share some cleaning tips

- Talk to them about how to choose accommodation e.g. weekly cost, distance from university

- Talk to them about finances e.g. apportioning money, looking for bargains in supermarkets, utility bills, student travel cards, overdrafts, the difference between debit and credit cards, and how to find more money (read Chapter 7: Money)

- Talk to them about how they might feel during the first term e.g. euphoric, sad, happy or overwhelmed - and they might experience all of those emotions at different times. Explain that the first term is likely to be hardest in terms of settling in but to keep going, if they can, and to seek help if they need it (read Chapter 9)

- Encourage them to read this book before they leave :-)

End Notes

Countdown to Leaving

UCAS https://www. www.ucas.com

Introduction

HESA. First year higher education (HE) student enrolments by level of study
https://www.hesa.ac.uk/data-and-analysis/sb252/figure-1

Chapter 1 - How Are You Feeling?

HESA. HE student enrolments by level of study, mode of study, domicile
and country of HE provider
https://www.hesa.ac.uk/data-and-analysis/sb252/figure-7

Chapter 2 - Important Things To Do Before The Start Of Term

Student Finance https://www.gov.uk/student-finance

The Tab. How much will freshers week cost at your uni?
https://thetab.com/2015/09/14/revealed-the-cost-of-freshers-week-53498

Chapter 3 - Living Away From Home: Your New Accommodation

HESA Student Record 2017/18, January 2019

University friends: By chance or by design? By Martin Rosenbaum Freedom
of information specialist @rosenbaum6 8th December 2018
https://www.bbc.co.uk/news/education-46430204

Chapter 5 - Food & Drink

NHS Eat Well Eating a Balanced Diet, 2019
https://www.nhs.uk/live-well/eat-well/

Chapter 6 - Friendships & Relationships

'Tea Consent' https://youtu.be/oQbei5JGiT8

Animation copyright Blue Seat Studios (www.blueseatstudios.com) and text
copyright Emmeline May (http://rockstardinosaurpirateprincess.com/)

NHS Contraception Guide. Emergency contraception (morning after pill,
IUD), 2018
https://www.nhs.uk/conditions/contraception/emergency-contraception/

Chapter 7 - Money

The National Student Money Survey 2019/www.savethestudent.org
https://www.savethestudent.org/money/student-budgeting/what-do-
students-spend-their-money-on.html

Gov.uk Student Finance – new full time students
https://www.gov.uk/student-finance/new-fulltime-students
NHSBSA NHS Low Income Scheme, NHSBSA Copyright 2019
https://www.nhsbsa.nhs.uk/nhs-low-income-scheme
NHSBSA Buy an NHS Prescription Prepayment Certificate, NHSBSA
    Copyright 2019
https://apps.nhsbsa.nhs.uk/ppc-online/patient.do
The Scholarship Hub https://www.thescholarshiphub.org.uk/blog/over-
    %C2%A3150-million-worth-of-scholarships-uk-students
Gov.uk. Higher and Degree Apprenticeships, 2019 https://www.gov.uk/
    government/publications/higher-and-degree-apprenticeships

Chapter 8 - Staying Safe At University

Ian Johnson, Chronicle Live, 28th December 2018 https://www.
    chroniclelive.co.uk/news/north-east-news/northumbri-university-
    newcastle-durham-initiation-15584472
Tony Diver and Georgia Gee, The Telegraph, 7th December 2018 https://
    www.telegraph.co.uk/news/2018/12/07/ucl-students-union-closes-
    controversial-mens-rugby-club-attempt
Vaping in England: evidence update summary February 2019
https://www.gov.uk/government/publications/vaping-in-england-an-
    evidence-update-february-2019/vaping-in-england-evidence-update-
    summary-february-2019

Chapter 9 - Feeling Sad, Worried, Overwhelmed, Lonely Or Worse

More Students Seek Mental Health Support, Analysis Shows by Grace
    Spitzer-Wong. BBC Shared Data Unit. 29 October 2018
https://www.bbc.co.uk/news/uk-england-45824598

Licences

About the Author

Melissa Scallan is a journalist and a researcher with a Master's degree in psychology from the London School of Economics. Melissa said goodbye to her eldest daughter in 2018 when she headed off to university. Her daughter returns home occasionally with giant bags of laundry

Acknowledgements

Particular thanks must go to Louise Salmon for her thoughtful editing and enthusiasm, Molly Shields for her positivity, her wonderful illustrations and for making this book look so fantastic, and to Karen McCormella Carter for her constant encouragement and marketing advice. And also to Mark, Katie and Ellie who've put up with me being focused on the book for the last 18 months.

Many, many people have helped me with this book. Family and good friends have given me encouragement, sent me relevant information, shared experiences, given me advice, forwarded the research questionnaire and proofread. And the organisations that I approached for advice and information have been so helpful and supportive too.

Thank you.

Printed in Great Britain
by Amazon